A Certain Life

Paul and Carol Alexander

INTEGRITY
MEDIA EUROPE

Integrity Media Europe
Unit 1 Hargreaves Business Park
Hargreaves Road
Eastbourne
BN23 6QW

www.integrityeurope.com
www.iworship24-7.com

ISBN 978-1-907080-18-0

Typeset by Richard Weaver
Printed and bound in the UK by CPI Anthony Rowe,
Chippenham and Eastbourne

Contents

Dedication

To our children, Anna and Jason,
who have enriched our lives and whom we love dearly.

What others are saying about
A Certain Life

"In this exciting and often moving account of two lives given over to the service of God, we learn theology from the unexpected twists and turns of the story. No Christian could fail to be touched by this book or fail to emerge wiser after reading it."

William Kay
Professor of Theology
Glyndŵr University, UK

"There are few things more compelling than biblical theology that has been earthed through practical application. In this readable and articulate work, Paul and Carol Alexander have captured a 'sound from heaven' and offered it to us as an echo that will resonate in the heart of everyone who reads it. It carries my wholehearted recommendation."

John Glass
General Superintendent, Elim Pentecostal Churches

"This book offers four highly valuable things money usually cannot buy:
… Rich life experiences
… Balanced theological wisdom
… Certain faith foundations
… and access to further study and help."

Stuart Bell
Senior Pastor New Life Lincoln and leader of the Ground Level Network of churches

Acknowledgements

A book like this could not have been written without countless experiences and the many people who have been woven into the fabric of each experience.

Firstly, thanks to the people at Integrity Media for publishing this work. Then to Tim Pettingale and Eldred Willey, for their encouragement and editorial assistance, we express our gratitude.

Secondly, we would like to thank our parents for what they invested in us. We both came from secure and loving homes and we honour Paul's late parents, Daniel and Yvonne Alexander, and Carol's parents, Audrey and Henry Malan.

There are countless colleagues and friends who must also be thanked. Some of the lecturers that we were blessed to sit under over thirty-six years ago have shaped our thoughts, lives and theology. The late John Carter and beloved John Philips must not go unmentioned. They impacted us in a profound way. There are many others, too numerous to mention, but their investment in our lives is appreciated. To Gerry and Mary Schoonbee who believed in us and in our vision we say thank you. To all the early pioneers that stood with us in the birthing of Africa School of Missions, our heartfelt thanks to each one of you for trusting two intrepid young people with only a vision and very little else to offer. You joined us in our venture and believed with us for a world that could be touched and changed by the transforming love of Christ. The early classes of students who trusted us with their training, we hold you in such high regard. We celebrate and marvel at the things that many of you have gone on to achieve.

We want to especially thank Carol's brother, Geoff Malan. In the early days of our faith ventures Geoff was our greatest support and ally. He was our children's surrogate Dad when their own Daddy had to serve in the military as a chaplain and when he went on overseas speaking engagements. Geoff invested into the lives of our children and into our vision. He is a true servant and we owe him so much.

We owe gratitude to those who work with us day by day. Our committed faculty and staff at Mattersey Hall College and Graduate School are a source of great encouragement. A special word of thanks to our personal assistant Ruth Brightwell, whose cheerful servanthood and attitude encourages us immensely. Our students at Mattersey and Africa School of Missions are also a constant inspiration.

Special thanks must go to our children, Anna and Jason. They have enriched us. Their love and commitment to us has blessed us more than they could realise. You will read about them in many of the pages of this book. Both of them have sacrificed with us in numerous ways so that the cause of the Gospel would extend to the nations of this world. We thank God for the loving relationship and friendship we share with them and our son-in-law Rich. Ava Carol (Anna and Rich's daughter) came into our world on the 21st of May, 2009. Our lives have never been the same – we feel blessed to have her. And added to this joy is the imminent arrival of her little brother at the end of January 2011. Our lives have been a rainbow of colour and our family is painted indelibly into every aspect.

Finally, we must thank our God who came into our lives when we were both young teenagers. He has blessed us from the moment we committed ourselves to become His followers. Never has He failed us or let us down. We are so thankful that He brought us into each other's lives when we were teenagers. He has blessed our marriage and we love each other more now than we ever have. We have never gone without and even in the darkest nights (and there have been quite a few!) He has been there. Life would be meaningless without Him – and this book would make no sense if He were not etched into every word on these pages. To Him we ascribe honour and glory and seek to serve Him with servant and willing hearts the remainder of our days.

Paul and Carol Alexander
Mattersey, Winter 2010

Foreword

There is a proverb that says, "the way of the wise winds upwards" and when I think of the path of life, full of twists and turns, whether due to unscheduled crises, huge disappointments, sudden opportunities, surprising miraculous provision or just the familiar interruptions of living in a world susceptible to the ridiculous and mundane, I think of the wisdom and wonder that have paved the path Paul and Carol have travelled thus far!

Saint Thomas Aquinas observed, "If the highest aim of a captain were to preserve his ship, he would keep it in port forever." If anything has marked the path travelled by these two incredible leaders it has been their relentless pursuit of the far horizon in obeying God's distinctive call on their lives. They have, on countless occasions, embarked on faith ventures irrespective of the cost, accompanied by generously severing any claim to legitimate material acquisitions or personal notoriety. Despite their many sacrifices they have seen God's goodness and mercy stalk them every step of the way – not least of which is the fruit of a worldwide ministry, but also the blessing of their family. Their children, who have sailed through so many of the storms and experienced the thrill of the open seas with them, to this day still rise up and call them blessed. Is there any greater fruit of wisdom?

We live in a world where so many intellectuals pursue a knowledge and understanding of God that is often far removed from the grit and grime of life in the trenches of faith. Then there are those heroic followers of Christ who throw themselves headlong into life's battles without being armed with theological depth and rigour. Paul and Carol have constantly bridged these two extremes and in chronicling their journey in *A Certain Life* inspire us to dig beneath the "form" of Christian living to discover the beauty and the power of the essence of a life wholeheartedly devoted to Jesus and His purposes.

Whoever you are, wherever you are headed, you are about to be motivated, moved and challenged to live a certain life. There is so much God knows about you that you have yet to discover as you enjoy the twists and turns that Paul and Carol wisely and faithfully navigated as pioneers, parents, principals, pastors and leaders in this life!

DJ McPhail
Senior Leader, Liberty Church
Randburg, South Africa

Preface

How To Read This Book

"The search for truth is more precious than its possession."
—Albert Einstein

"I am the way the truth and the life."
—Jesus

It is our hope that this book will help many. It is important for you to be able to get the best from reading it, so here are some things to watch for.

Firstly, this book is a form of *practical theology*. In other words, it uses narrative and explanation to help you discover the nature and character of God. Developing a comprehensive theology that is not protective and defensive, or shallow and superficial, is a very important part of growing as a Christian. God chose several thousand years, the stories of hundreds and three languages (Hebrew, Greek and Aramaic) to reveal Himself through the Bible. Additionally, we have a complex history of the Church and its practices and beliefs that spans many nations and cultures and two millennia. It is now up to us to put all the pieces together and develop a positive understanding of the grace, love and forgiveness of God in our lives and contexts. Look in these pages for these theological insights and try to develop a thorough and comprehensive understanding of just who God is.[1]

Then, there are parts of this book that provide commentary. For centuries Christian scholars (and Jewish scholars before them) have written down their own insights regarding the Bible. We call these collected insights commentaries. Although this book does not set out to expound any particular part of the Bible, from time to time we give our insights into Bible

verses. We do not try to make the Bible conform to our experience, quite the opposite, we make sure that our experience
conforms to the Bible. Time and time again we have proven
the amazing wisdom of God's Word and we use these pages to
illustrate this.

Throughout this book we use endnoting. This is primarily
an academic tool to help people read the text in an informed
way. Then we go one step further. Reading a book should be a
kind of introduction to other friends who share on similar
subjects, either in more detail or with greater insight. So, we
use endnotes to introduce you to our friends and we hope that
you enjoy the adventure of meeting them. You will encounter
numbers of good authors and books that can help you take the
journey we initiate with you much further. These are all books
that we have valued in our own journey and we trust will
inspire and help you too. Make sure that you do not gloss over
the footnotes. They are not just added extras – they are sign-
posts for the journey. Sometimes we give specific references.
This is to allow you to quickly look up the particular subject
that those pages are dealing with. At other times we simply
give you an introduction to the book as a whole.

This book is also devotional. In other words, we are hoping
to inspire you to love God and to love life more. We want to
give you hope and courage.[2] This is very important to us. It is a
constant theme of ours as we travel the world and share in
various situations. We would like to think that you will read
this book with an open heart and be ready to be challenged
and helped. It might be that you would like to use each one of
the principles shared as a devotional theme and to work
through some specific application of the principle in your own
life over a period of time.

Then, you should note the structure of the book. It is not
intended as an autobiographical work. Although our story or

narrative runs throughout, the intention is to describe theological thought in a practical way. Thus, the stories that you read are not in any kind of chronological order. There is, however a natural progression. Firstly, we introduce you to the principles that have helped us in laying foundations. These are the big building blocks of life. We have discovered that these principles have become non-negotiables in our lives. They are our default position. Decisions, relationships and future plans are almost always matched with these principles and if they are out of sync, we realise very early on that whatever we are thinking or planning probably won't work. Then we progress to principles that apply to the journey of life. These are axioms that work again and again and illustrate the gracious character and nature of God as He works. We endeavour to develop a theological foundation for a certain and secure future. In other words, we hope that the principles that are developed through the later stages of the book will help you take confident steps into your own future and, importantly, determine to sustain your Christ-following passion for the remainder of your life. These are principles that we continue to hone and develop so that we will make our children and their children rightly proud. These are lifestyle choices that impact upon our leadership and our long-term view of life.

Finally, a word about the title of this book. The word "certain" is ambiguous in the sense that it can mean different things to different people. The choice of the word was intentional and we do deliberately play on the word. Certain can mean "to know for sure" or "a particular way of knowing". For us the word means both. We are living a particular and certain life, which is that of committed Christ-followers. It also means we live it with a sense of certainty and know without a doubt that we have chosen, "the way, the truth and the life". Our hearts are certain of this!

May you enjoy your journey through the pages of this book as we share our lives with you as transparently as we know how. We have always sought to live the principles over a long period before we share them. Thus, we determined to raise our kids before we had too much to say about parenting. We have tried to lead with integrity before we spoke too boldly about how to lead. We have always been committed to love each other passionately in order to write out of a wholesome and complete marriage. Consequently, the writing of this book has been a happy process. We have not robbed our kids of time as we have spent long hours in writing. We have not had to wrestle with our thoughts and motives constantly enquiring about why we are writing. We have simply reached the happiest season of our lives where God has taught us much. We have dealt positively with pain and we celebrate being alive. We hope that this happy and uncomplicated faith will impact you as you read on.

Endnotes

1. Two books we have found useful in this regard are: R. R. Osmer, *Practical Theology: An Introduction* (Grand Rapids, MI: Eerdmans, 2008), and R. S. Anderson, *The Shape of Practical Theology: Empowering Ministry with Theological Praxis* (Downers Grove, IL: Waveland Press Inc, 2002). Anderson offers a useful definition of practical theology: "…practical theology is a dynamic process of reflective, critical inquiry into the praxis of the church in the world and God's purposes for humanity, carried out in the light of Christian Scripture and tradition, and in critical dialogue with other sources of knowledge." p22. In other words, practical theology considers theory and praxis equally – not one or the other. It takes into account the truth of human experience.

2. On the topic of hope we suggest T. Wright, *Surprised by Hope* (London: SPCK, 2007).

A Certain Life

*Principles for Life and
Leading*

"We shall not cease from exploration
And the end of all our exploring
Will be to arrive where we started
And know the place for the first time."
—T.S Eliot, *Little Gidding*

*"… and if you look for it [wisdom] as for silver and search for it
as hidden treasure, then you will understand the fear of the Lord
and find the knowledge of God."*
(Proverbs 2:4-5)

This book had a most undignified start. We were on one of numerous plane trips when our conversation became quite animated. We had just concluded a time of speaking to younger leaders and began to realise that we were passing on well-tried principles for life and living that had increasingly become a part of the fabric of our lives, but which had taken many years to learn. The enthusiastic response of our listeners suggested that we were on to something. We spoke to each other rapidly, trying to remember all that we had shared. Carol then frantically started looking around for a piece of paper to scribble down the thoughts that we were excitedly sharing with each other. In the absence of an alternative, the first notes for this book were written on the back of an airsick bag! However, we have treasured that bag and its scribbled notes and in the pages that follow we hope that you will be helped and inspired by these simple, yet helpful, principles for life and living. There is something so rewarding about living a *certain* life.

We did not always have this perspective. Although both of us enjoyed very stable homes and our childhoods were relatively uncluttered, that soon changed after we both became committed Christ-followers. Our love for Christ quite quickly introduced us to the world of Christian service and it was not long before we were spending most of our Saturdays with kids in a very socially deprived part of our home city, Johannesburg. This led to leadership in our church youth group and it was not long before we were leaving home and country for Bible College in the UK.

Although the pace of decision-making in those innocent young days bore us along without us ever being conscious of anxiety or worry, we soon began to realise that life is not just a succession of spontaneous decisions and a bit of good luck. Our exposure to Bible teaching made us aware of the bigness of the God we had chosen to serve and how He makes Himself known to His children. At times, the harsh financial realities of trying to achieve our dreams made us realise that life was not always simple. Our happy naivety was being stripped away and we had several choices as to what would replace it.

The first choice was to develop an ill-considered confidence, believing that somehow God would always do just what we wanted Him to. If we believed, then surely God was somehow bound by His promises to respond to our faith? In some ways this view seemed completely reasonable and we noticed many of our friends and colleagues adopting this perspective. There was vibrancy about these people who seemed to have limitless faith for almost anything. Bigger houses, better cars and successful lives were all a part of this option, but instinctively we felt there was something missing. What if things did not work out as we believed? Whose fault was that? Was God not hearing for some reason? An initial response to these questions suggested that the most obvious reason seemed to lie within us. If we encountered some restriction in the spiritual or material areas of our lives what would be the cause? Could it be some secret or un-confessed problem? Was there an issue from our past? These questions provided no satisfying answers either practically or theologically. And so, over a period of time, we discarded the triumphalist, "God will always do what we ask" flavour of faith.[3] This theological perspective could not be reconciled with that of someone living a certain life that was based upon a clear and satisfying knowledge of the kindness, goodness and providence of an eternal God who was committed to our well-being in every circumstance of life.

The second choice was even less appetising. It was a kind of cynical, almost critical view of life and faith. We became aware of Christian leaders who seemed to be "against" almost everything and "for" almost nothing. Their language was aggressive, suggesting that somehow we needed to fight for the faith that was given to our fathers and that, if we did not, true faith would disappear from the earth in our lifetime. We almost immediately found this strange faith atmosphere dampened any level of enthusiasm that we had for life. Growing up as a Christian leader was getting harder! We had no idea that it could be so complicated and that so many people who claimed to be honest and passionate about their faith could take sides and defend their view so aggressively. Paul remembers arriving at church in his late teens to find a bitter altercation going in the foyer between a deacon and one of the church members over whether to admit the man's wife who had chosen to come to church without a head covering. It was deemed important for women to cover their heads in church in those days, but it seemed to be the reason for drawing invisible battle lines between those of pure (even biblical?) faith and those of lesser devotion. We soon tired of this kind of church life and kept hoping for something better.[4]

So was there a middle line or a better way? To be honest, this uncomplicated and happy expression of faith seemed so hard to find. In fact, it took us years to find that place where the heart can sing and the spirit is made glad and God becomes the centre of a deep and uncomplicated devotion. Part of the journey was theological. In other words, we had to work out how we related to God. We knew that we came to God through the amazing redemptive work of Jesus Christ, but understanding His character and nature seemed a much more complicated process. Was His will for my life to be discovered through demanding devotion that relied heavily upon mystically dis- cerning His way? Was it merely practical, requiring little more than good common sense? It was in trying to get answers to these questions that we began, slowly at first, to find principles that were both theologically sound and highly practical.[5] But, we are running ahead of ourselves. Perhaps an account of one of our very early experiences will help set the scene for the remainder of this book.

Soon after leaving Bible college we found ourselves invited to speak in churches, youth groups and school assemblies in different countries. We started in the UK and soon found our- selves crossing the US as well. Some of our stories will be found in other parts of this book. We eventually made our way from San Francisco to Honolulu, Hawaii. Who wouldn't want to do this kind of thing? Of course it was exciting, but we were trying to serve God in all of this. Our passion to please Him was high and so we did not want to get things wrong. Our

training and early Christian development had taught us to seek
God's will earnestly. We knew that doing exactly what God
wanted us to do was the most important thing in all the world.
Every decision was supported with much prayer. We read the
Bible to find words that would suggest that God was happy
with our decisions. Every sermon was interpreted as to whether
this was God confirming our plans or blocking our plans. We
honestly and passionately believed in an interventionist God
who could and should direct every step that we ever took.

Whilst in Hawaii we devoted long periods of time to prayer
and, very often, we fasted as well. This method of finding
God's plan for our lives had made us fastidious about fulfilling
the disciplines that our early leaders had suggested were all a
part of living in a God-pleasing way. During one of these
rather passionate prayer times, Paul felt a distinct impression
that God wanted us to go to Samoa. What was confusing
about this impression was that neither of us had the faintest
idea where Samoa was nor whether, in fact, there was even a
place with that name! We found an atlas at the local library and
soon located a number of little islands just south of the equator
called Samoa. This seemed to confirm that God was at work in
leading and directing us and we began to believe that He could
possibly open an opportunity to get us there.

Of course we could not help talking excitedly about our new
sense of God's leading and within a day or two a local pastor
told us that he knew a missionary in American Samoa who, he
thought, would be glad to hear from us. He supplied us with
his name and address and we wrote an enthusiastic note telling
him of our sense of God's leading and that we could assist with
children's work, Bible studies and preaching in local churches.
We earnestly anticipated the reply but were sorely disappointed
when it came. This missionary told us in no uncertain terms
that we were not welcome and should not bother to come. To

add to our disappointment he told us that others had gone on mission to him before only to enjoy the tropical island and not to do any form of Christian work. We were devastated. Again, the issue of knowing God's will for our lives was proving so complicated! Had we been taught incorrectly? Was there something wrong with us? So, we resorted to the things we knew to do: more prayer, fasting and Bible reading. Incredibly, we were left with the same firm conviction: we were to go to Samoa!

With a sense of great obedience to God we took our meagre savings, spent all of our resources and bought two tickets for a little island, which was one mile wide and twenty-seven miles long in the middle of the Pacific Ocean. It soon dawned upon us that the flight we boarded in Honolulu was arriving in the Samoan capital of Pago Pago at the terrible hour of 1.00 am. What were we to do? Our obedience had made us take the journey, but now we were arriving at an unearthly hour, knowing no one and having virtually no resources to even catch a bus into town. Again we began to pray! Carol prayed for a Christian taxi driver who would let us sleep in the back of his car. Paul began to imagine how he would one day tell his relatively new father-in-law how it was that he had managed to get his daughter stranded on Robinson Crusoe's island.

And so we arrived. The air was balmy and tropical and we were met with Islander fanfare and tiki lamps. As we made our way out of the little arrivals hall Paul noticed a rather ancient bus parked nearby. It seemed to be going somewhere and so he suggested that we catch it, if only to pass another hour or two. After loading our two small cases onto the back of the bus he took his seat next to Carol who asked if he had seen the nice couple standing outside the arrivals hall. She was convinced they were Christians, but what difference did that make to us? Carol quickly suggested that Paul bury his pride and ask the couple who they were waiting for. What a ridiculous suggestion!

However, her feminine way prevailed and soon Paul was leaving the bus, asking the driver not to drive away and walked to where this nice couple was standing. He asked them who they were waiting for and nearly fainted when they said that they were hoping to see Paul and Carol Alexander! Introductions quickly took place and a rather proud husband, who was revelling in his confidence, beckoned Carol off the bus. It was not long before we had retrieved our cases, placed them on the back of a little pick-up truck and the four of us were heading towards Pago Pago in the very early hours of the morning.

This couple's story was as amazing as ours. They had worked on the island for several years and had often prayed for an opportunity to build good relationships with the leadership of the Congregational Churches, which were the most numerous of all denominations in Samoa. After many closed doors a senior minister from these churches eventually approached them asking for help with their children's work. This was not this couple's strength and they felt devastated that they could not provide a more positive response. It happened that at almost exactly this time they went to collect their post from the boxes at the main post office. Whilst there they met another missionary who had also just collected his mail. He had chosen to open one that had been postmarked "Honolulu". It was our letter! Soon the missionary was complaining out loud, asking who this Paul and Carol Alexander thought they were! Why did they want to come to the island? He had no need of children's workers! We can only believe that God orchestrated the timing of this whole event.

Our friends began to pray about what they had heard and wondered if we could be a part of the answer in terms of the request from the leaders of the Congregational Churches. Like us, they felt an inner conviction that we were still coming and felt that they should get to the airport on that particular early morning, believing that they would find us. How amazing! We went on to enjoy wonderful success with children across the island, speaking to hundreds. We also found open doors into many churches and spent the next month preaching, speaking and encouraging leaders. It is a wonderful story that helped lay principles into our lives that have assisted us in living a certain life.

We share this story to demonstrate that the will of God can be found in different ways. In our early days of ministry we prayed, fasted and read the Bible carefully in the hope of hearing God's voice and finding His will. As we have grown in our faith we have found that there are other important principles that help us to honour God and live well. There are times when we do not need to go through the long and, at times, agonising processes that we went through as young leaders. However, learned lessons and established principles, like proverbs and wise maxims, can also play a major role in discerning God's best for us. These principles form the central theme of the book you now have in your hands.[6]

The years have past and we have made some wrong and painful choices in that time. Happily, however, our theological journeys blended with living now combine to present us with the most enjoyable season of life ever. We have lived on four continents. We have led great churches and several excellent ministry-training colleges. We speak around the world each year. We are parents to grown children and have recently had the joy of becoming grandparents. It is dawning on us that we have learnt some principles that are consistent with the Bible and reveal the amazing character of God that are central to living a certain life.

We hope to share principles and stories throughout this book that will help many prevent making some of the painful mistakes we have made in our journey through life. We also hope to enrich your understanding of the amazing and gracious God who is revealed in the Bible. We hope that we will enable you to enjoy reading your Bible understanding how and why it was written. All of this is to one end: seeing as many as possible who call themselves Christ-followers living well, enjoying God and celebrating a certain life.

Endnotes

3. Two books that could be helpful in this regard are: R.E. Webber, *Ancient Future Faith: Rethinking Evangelicalism for a Postmodern World* (Grand Rapids: Baker Books, 1999). R. E. Webber, *The Younger Evangelicals: Facing the Challenges of the New World* (Grand Rapids: Baker Books, 2002).
4. See the discussion on fundamentalism in Osmer, *Practical Theology*, pp. 153-155. Webber, *Younger Evangelicals*, pp23-70 expounds the shift in evangelicalism over the past century and the era of evangelical fundamentalism.
5. N.T. Wright, *The Challenge of Jesus* (London: SPCK, 2000), pp15-16 deals with some of the theological challenges confronting the leadership task.
6. Anderson, *The Shape of Practical Theology*, pp40-46 deals with some of praxis of leadership.

Time and Space

Testing the Will of God

"Act and God will act."
—Joan of Arc

"I know God will not give me anything I cannot handle.
I just wish He didn't trust me so much."
—Mother Teresa of Calcutta

*"Therefore, I urge you, brothers, in view of God's mercy, to offer
your bodies as living sacrifices, holy and pleasing to God – this is
your spiritual act of worship ... Then you will be able to test and
approve what God's will is – His good, pleasing and perfect will."*
(Romans 12:1-2)

We will speak often throughout this book of the unique relationship that Christ-followers enjoy with God. This involves sensing His presence, praying about our needs, worshipping out of gratitude and seeking His will for our lives. Any person who sincerely devotes their life to follow Jesus will gladly and willingly tell you about these enriching experiences of faith just as we do.

As thrilling as a life of faith can be, however, there is a constant tension that God's people have faced throughout the centuries. It is the difficult interface between our limited dimension of time and space and God's infinite dimension of eternity. Most people who love God and passionately serve Him will be willing to share about those difficult times when the promise that they feel God has given them about a particular situation and the fulfilment of that promise are separated by an agonisingly long period of time. This gap between a clear sense of God's will for our lives and the actual fulfilment of that promise has been in focus in the lives of the people of God since the earliest of times.

Two things are abundantly clear as we try to grasp the way in which the Bible describes this journey of faith in testing the will of God for our lives. The first is that God's people do not rely upon good luck. One of the differentiating marks of a Christ-follower is the ability to exercise trust and confidence in the intrinsic goodness of a great God, without resorting to superstition or relying upon a stroke of good luck. God does not require His people to be fatalistic, living with anxiety and fear. Thus, the New Testament part of the Bible makes it clear that God is in control and that He is able to orchestrate our lives in such a way that everything ultimately works together for our good.[7] In the story of Joseph in the Old Testament, the end of the story reveals that what his brothers had meant for his harm had actually been for everyone's good.[8] In other words, we have a theology that never views God as some kind of distant potentate who does not intervene in the events of our lives, leaving us to some kind of indeterminate fate. Christian theology strongly accepts the gracious working of an involved God in the smallest details of our lives.[9]

The second thing that is clear from the biblical record is that we should never resort to divination of any kind. This means that we do not seek to somehow engage the unseen or spirit world through mediums or diviners. The Bible refers to this as witchcraft and suggests that the whole practice is manipulative, controlling, deceptive and confusing. Thus, Christians should refuse the suggestion that our destiny and future is somehow available through the alignment of the stars, a shadow in a crystal ball or the placement of a tarot card. We certainly do not believe in hearing voices from beyond the grave and we understand that there is a dark world with evil spirits that can easily confuse or mislead people.[10]

The position of Christ-followers is one that fervently and steadfastly declares that God is not a man, therefore He does not lie or cheat and neither does He tempt or tease.[11] It is not in the character of God to dangle us over a flame to see how much we can take. He never, note, *never* places evil before us just to see how strong we might be in resisting the temptation to do what is clearly wrong.[12]

So, having established that God's people are not the kind that resort to good luck and superstition or to divination and spiritism, just what is it that we believe regarding discerning the way and will of God? It is important to establish just what Christian people *do* believe in terms of testing the will of God, whilst living within the confines of time and space.

The most important element in our testing of God's will comes back to our deep rooted belief in the character of God. The Bible is not just a collection of words or sayings, it is a story written over centuries. It is significant that when God gave us His word as a guide to our lives that He dedicated large swathes of it to narrative or story telling. We are able to trace the journey of families and even nations over long periods of time. We gain insights into special events, but we are also told of the normal rhythm and routine of life that people lived. This is important. Our faith is not based on a code of what is permissible and what is not permissible. It is based upon the story of God's involvement with His people. An analysis of this God-involvement will show the consistency of His character.

He is slow to anger and abundant in mercy![13] He is the same yesterday, today and forever![14] He does not change with the seasons or withhold good gifts from His people.[15] Anyone who sincerely reads the Bible will discover the revelation of a kind and gracious God who dearly loves those He has created.[16]

This theological fact alone allows us to rest in the midst of the worst of circumstances knowing that God will not leave us and, should comfort be needed, He will comfort us.[17] One of the earliest stories ever told about God is the Old Testament book called Job. Without the benefit of any written Scripture, Job was navigating his way through the most difficult of circumstances. His humanity and pain are more than evident, but a bright light shines through the whole story. Job concludes that it is the Lord who gives and the Lord who takes away, but God is so true that regardless of the outcome His name is to be praised. This is not some form of fatalistic helplessness – this is a high and confident faith in the eternal God who sees far beyond our world that is so limited by time and space, and plans the lives of His children in a way that ultimately will be the very best.

Then there is the whole concept and practice of prayer. When it comes to finding God's best for our lives there is a huge catalogue in the Bible of how and when we should pray. Jesus Himself is very clear in this area. He prayed and He taught us to pray. He taught us to pray that the Father's will might be done on earth in the same way that it is done in heaven.[18] In other words, that the eternal perspective of our Father might be accomplished within the confines of our time-bound lives. Jesus also taught us to pray with faith, believing that we can trust God to accomplish His will. He suggested that we should be like a woman in deep need who would knock and keep on knocking until the person who could meet her need responded.[19] In other words, there is the sense that we hold tenaciously to what we believe to be God's will for our lives until such time as the answer comes. However else we view the role of prayer in our lives, a significant element of praying is to enable our lives to span the gap between time and eternity and live positive, faith-filled lives believing in the promise of a gracious and loving God.

Further to our knowledge of the consistent character and nature of God, as well as the important role of prayer in discerning the will of God, there is what the Bible calls the *internal umpire.* This is the peace which God can give that goes beyond our normal sense of understanding and rules in our hearts like an umpire.[20] When circumstances scream impossibility to us there is the clear sound of the umpire's whistle.[21] Sometimes the umpire can see things that players never can and when the whistle blows you know there is another perspective that is wider and greater than the one you have in the field of play. Thousands of Christ-followers will tell of the amazing sense of tranquillity that overrules the natural and allows Christians the peace of knowing that God is working out a situation in His time and way. We know that He makes everything beautiful in His time.[22]

There is one further element to testing the will of God. In order to understand it, a recap of the previous three paragraphs will be helpful. Testing the will of God is dependent upon our commitment to the *character* of God as we have learnt it from the Bible. Then there is the importance of *prayer* and thirdly, the *inner peace* and strength we can have that is evidence of the fact that God is at work in our lives. The fourth component to testing the will of God is *patience* mixed with a good degree of tenacity and *courage.* As the character and nature of God impact our lives and His truth is deposited within our hearts, we can anticipate internal change. There is a grace that takes us beyond the personality type that we have developed, beyond the preconditioning of our lives (including disappointment and hurt) and places within us a confident and courageous disposition. This must not be confused with arrogance or self-confidence. This grace is never boastful or abrasive. Rather, it is a quiet, internal strength that enables us to keep going, keep trusting and keep certain in the face of circumstances that appear completely different to what we might have hoped or even prayed for. God's character as described in the Bible, prayer, His peace in our hearts and a deep seated courage and tenacity all combine to enable the Christ-follower to patiently test and prove the will of God for their lives. This is what the Bible refers to as offering ourselves as living sacrifices, completely, so that we might prove the good and acceptable will of God.[23]

We began to discover these principles from the earliest times of our Christ-following adventure. Shortly after we met and began courting we responded to the challenge to volunteer for a summer children's programme organised by our local church. It used material from a well-known children's ministry and the weeklong program was called "Vacation Bible School". We loved being with the kids, though we were only in our teens ourselves. Many children from a rather socially and economically deprived part of town attended that week and it was evident that their lives had been deeply impacted. It seemed only natural to us to ask what would be done for them once the special week was over. To our amazement it seemed as though no one had given this a thought. They mainly came from dysfunctional homes, so it was unlikely that many of their parents or guardians would go to the trouble of taking them to Sunday School. To us it seemed as though the effort of the week would be wasted if there were not some form of follow up.

Thus it was that we decided to start a children's outreach program in the area where most of the children came from. We naively thought that everyone would want to be a part of this exciting initiative, but soon found that no one in our own church shared our excitement. The church leaders seemed particularly disinterested and that disturbed us. They suggested that they were happy for us to do whatever we felt led to do, but not to expect support of any kind.

We knew that there was a church closer to where the children lived. We had actually conducted one or two of the Vacation Bible School sessions there, so we made an appointment to meet with the Pastor and seek his help as well as the use of the church. We met him some days later and were quietly horrified when he told us that the church was not available as the children would probably ruin the carpets! As very young and impressionable Christians this did not seem to be making sense.

So one of our first battles in proving and testing the will of God began. We questioned whether we were just being over-enthusiastic, and whether the whole project was unrealistic. We questioned the issue of submitting to local church authority. Although we were not told not to do what we had planned, we were surprised and even hurt that our own church leadership was not more encouraging. We had both just started work and between us earned barely more than our expenses with little to spare. How would we finance this project? These and many similar questions are typical of the struggle to find God's will and reconcile the eternal world with the limitations of time and space.

As we prayed together, however, we felt undeterred by the setbacks we had suffered. Although we could not describe it well back then, we were exercising a deliberate and tenacious courage in the face of discouragement. We shared internal feelings with each other, prayed much and often, and again and again we were left with the distinct impression that we had to do all in our power to reach out to these children whom we had come to love so much.

So it was that we took the decision to begin looking around the area for a suitable place to meet. We drove up and down several streets and there seemed no possible option. We returned to the street where the church was located and looked enviously at the space the building provided, knowing that it was not available. At that moment, we noticed a car parked across the street with a sticker on the bumper displaying a Christian message. We parked our car and went to the door of the house where the car was parked. A Chinese gentleman answered the door and was quick to invite us in. Although he spoke limited English we soon discovered that he was indeed a committed Christian. He insisted on offering us refreshments and we began sharing our own journey and talking about why we were in the area. Within minutes he suggested to us that we use the double garage beneath his house. He took us downstairs and we immediately saw the potential. He had a small printing press there, but we were able to cover it with a sheet. A week later we were given a large piece of carpet and within about ten days we were able to announce the start of a Good News Club in the heart of the area that we had felt so strongly led to.

That first Saturday morning was so exciting. Children poured in from around the area. We began teaching little songs, had memory verses and worked hard at preparing and delivering stories. Each week we would spend hours preparing attendance charts and visual aids. It was not long before we were asked to visit some of the children in their homes. Some lived in very sad places with broken and dysfunctional families and homes. Others came from homes where both parents worked hard but remained relatively poor. It became apparent that we were their only contact with Christ-following people. We were invited to share the good news of Christ's love with them and there was almost no resistance to us praying. When children were admitted to hospital we were often almost the only ones to visit them. Week after week we found an open door into needy homes and scores of boys and girls sang God-songs with us each Saturday morning.

We had proved the will of God, but for young people it was a difficult and discouraging process. The very people who should have supported us did not. There was no financial resource and no obvious place to hold our children's club. But the combined effect of prayer, inner peace and a courageous commitment resulted in a wide open door and many lives positively impacted for Christ.

We later attended Bible College and found that these formative experiences served us well. Soon doors opened to lead children's ministries in various places resulting in still further doors for preaching. Thus, in some ways, the pattern for our ministry throughout the years was set.

The Certain Life is not defined by endless success and complete provision for every aspect of life. It is often filled with challenges and even struggles. Again and again the tension between knowing the will and way of God and seeing that fulfilled is present. The eternal and the temporal sometimes take time to interface. But the principles are always the same. We never resort to good luck or some form of spiritual superstition. We trust in the goodness of our eternal Heavenly Father who delights to lead and direct us and never teases us. We likewise sustain the discipline of prayer and learn to discern the peace of God within our souls. Without arrogance or self-reliance we knock on doors, we keep courageous, we look for opportunities, knowing that He who began a good work in us will bring that to fruition. Those blessed with certain lives celebrate both the uniqueness of the plans of God for them as well as the achievement of God through them. Proving and testing the will of God reminds us of our humanity, but the provision and plans of God fulfilled through us remind us of

His greatness and goodness. We choose to live no other life but a *certain* life.

Endnotes

7. Colossians 1:17: *"He is before all things, and in Him all things hold together."* See also Romans 8:28
8. Genesis 50:20: *"You intended to harm me, but god intended it for good to accomplish what is now being done, the saving of many lives."*
9. Philippians 1:6, 2:13; 1 Corinthians 1:8
10. Exodus 22:18; Leviticus 20:27; 1 Samuel 28
11. Numbers 23:19
12. 1 Corinthians 10:13, 7:5; Hebrews 2:18, 4:14-16; James 1:13
13. Exodus 34:6; Deuteronomy 4:31; Nehemiah 9:31
14. Hebrews 13:8
15. 1 Samuel 15:29, Psalm 110:4; Malachi 3:6
16. John 3:16
17. Psalm 23:4, 119:76; Zechariah 1:17; Isaiah 49:13, 51:12; 2 Corinthians 1:4, 7:6
18. Matthew 6:5-15
19. Matthew 7:7-8
20. Philippians 4:7
21. Matthew 19:26; Mark 9:23, 10:27
22. Ecclesiastes 3:11, 8:6
23. Romans 12:1-2

Even in the Resurrection

Living with eternity in our hearts

"There is a God-shaped vacuum in the heart of every man
which cannot be filled by any created thing, but only by God,
the Creator, made known through Jesus."
—Blaise Pascal

*"He has also set eternity in the hearts of men; yet they cannot
fathom what God has done from beginning to end."*
(Ecclesiastes 3: 11)

From the time that we become Christ-followers we enter the
awkward world of living across two planes: time and eternity.
We find ourselves in the "now" but have a vocabulary and
expectation that describes the "not yet". Sometimes this experience stretches us as we decide exactly how to navigate the
challenges of life, especially issues such as death and sickness.

In fact, this issue of living a life of faith within the constricts
of time and space has been one faced by every successive gener-
ation of Christians. Some of the New Testament was written to
help people keep faith in the face of persecution, giving the
assurance that Christ would come again and that every bit of
suffering in the present would fade away in the splendour of
living with Him in eternity.

Some of the earliest controversies within the first few centuries of Church history related to the issue of bridging time and eternity. A group called the Gnostics struggled to understand the place of the human soul in a fallen and corrupt world. One group suggested that, just as an ingot of gold could not be contaminated if dropped into pigswill, so our souls cannot be contaminated by anything that we do with our bodies. This was a most convenient position for those who enjoyed licence to do almost anything, knowing that the "flesh" would not contaminate the soul. Others were not so sure. They decided that the best thing to do was to suppress the flesh in order to preserve the soul – thus restraining the appetites of their humanity, even to the point where physical mutilation became considered the noble thing to do.[24] How difficult this issue of living in time with the expectation of eternity was proving to be!

Within a few hundred years of the New Testament era people found this tension so hard to manage that they chose to hide away in monasteries or become "holy men" known as ascetics. It was clearly easier to exit the demands of daily living in a corrupt and fallen world than to find a vibrant faith by which to live in it.

This trend continued but often took more sinister forms. By the 11th Century the Church was not sure if its primary message was about eternity or about establishing powerful empires on earth that could somehow fulfil the Lord's prayer of "Your Kingdom come on earth as it is in heaven." The result of this misplaced theology was devastating, resulting in several Crusades led by Christian kings against the Muslims who, by this time, had taken control of Jerusalem and the Holy Land. Thousands marched to their death in the name of establishing God's kingdom on earth. Almost anything was condoned in order that the end result might be achieved. More Jews were slaughtered during the Crusades than were killed in the Nazi holocaust. Almost everyone and anyone became disposable in the name of the cause and the bitterness of the battle with the Islamic world remains a part of the political landscape to this day.

By the 12th Century most of Europe was a part of the new Empire and the Church took responsibility to govern every part of people's lives from the cradle to the grave. Sophisticated theological systems were developed in the name of the Pope with scant reference to early Church practice. It was decided that the souls of the departed could not enter heaven without a period of purification or purgatory – the place of purging. Intriguingly, the way to escape purgatory was to pay specific Church authorities, who by this stage had authority even over the souls of those departed. Some monastic orders became incredibly wealthy through little else but receiving a reward for praying and lighting candles for the dead. The bridging of the temporal and the eternal world had become the domain of superstition, manipulation and control.[25]

The Reformation in the fifteen hundreds was partly initiated by a reaction to the practice of selling indulgences. This practice allowed the Church to enrich itself by guaranteeing that the soul of a loved one would be immediately released from purgatory to the splendours of heaven upon the payment of a sum of money. Understandably there were many who found this practice very disturbing and, due to this and a number of other factors, the Reformation was born. However, the Reformers found the tension of living as people of faith this side of eternity just as challenging as their more superstitious opponents. Some believed that the way forward was through maintaining a highly disciplined lifestyle. People were valued not so much because of who they were but because of what they did. Although this had positive economic implications, it diminished the value of a person to the level of his or her contribution to society.

We still speak of the Protestant work ethic that, in a subtle way, has its roots in the tension we have discovered: how do we manage our lives as people of faith this side of eternity?

Some of the sons of the Reformers took the issue of dealing with the "flesh" even further. They considered every human appetite to be intrinsically evil. The most obvious of these was sex, which was not to be enjoyed on any account lest it somehow contaminate the soul. There are reports that the Puritans took this to such an extent that they covered the legs of pianos because they were deemed to be suggestive and seductive![26]

As if all this was not complicated enough, there was the issue of sickness and suffering. Christian theology is essentially the way in which we try to describe the character, attributes and acts of God. Without any hesitation, virtually all the variant forms of Christian theology would place the love of God at the top of every list. He is love in His very essence. All that He does is because He loves. But, the problem is that our high view of the love of God creates a huge conflict.[27] How can a loving God allow suffering and sickness? One cursory response is to blame everything that is bad on the Devil and attribute everything that is good to God. But what is our response when bad things happen to good people? Simply blaming the Devil seems so trite and superficial. Thus, the same problem arises yet again. How do we reconcile the present with eternity? How do we live with eternity in our hearts and death in our veins all at the same time?

This issue continues to dominate the theological machinations of the contemporary Church. On the concerning side of the issue is the tendency for us to continue to perpetuate superstitious practices in order to try and make sense of our existence in time. We have been aware for years of people who make offers of healing based upon a donation and the provision of a special bottle of "holy water" or a piece of anointed cloth. It is intriguing that most of these offers come with conditions relating to the sick person's ongoing involvement with a specific ministry or other. We have had to help troubled people who have gone through the trauma of some form of exorcism or "deliverance" ministry because it has been discerned that this is the root cause of their illness. Others we know of have gone through intricate ceremonies of anointing their cars with oil in an attempt to ensure protection on the roads. In one case we were aware of people pouring communion juice on the ground followed by the crumbs of bread from the communion table in order to "sanctify" the ground! Stating things as kindly as we know how, this is superstitious practice and has no precedent in either the Bible or in a comprehensive theology that embraces the whole scope of God's revelation to us. However, in an effort to understand these strange distortions of Christian theology the underlying problem is the same. How can we receive the promises and graces of a loving God whilst living in a fallen and dangerous world?

Thankfully, a very early experience in Paul's life has helped us in navigating this extremely challenging aspect of our Christ-following lives. Having grown up in a good but rather stoic Presbyterian household, Paul was invited to attend a vibrant church of the Pentecostal variety. It was all a bit strange, but rather attractive at the same time. It was the practice in that church to issue appeals for people to respond to the call to become a Christian and receive Christ as their personal Saviour. Paul had a particularly devoted friend who suggested in no uncertain terms that this was the right thing to do and so, knowing little of what he was actually committing to, Paul's hand went up and he was ushered forward to the front of the church to be prayed for. Following many expressions of happiness by his friends, Paul was assured that he was now a Christian and that everything would change and joy would flood his life.

Remarkably, things did begin to change. Within months the Bible began to make sense, worship was a reality, values were changing and this was followed by numerous little changes in the way Paul behaved and treated other people. He had begun the lifelong journey of being a Christ-follower.

Being just a young teenager he approached his parents about leaving the rather stayed Presbyterian church he had grown up in and joining this new, vibrant church which had helped him to discover a recognisable faith. Wisely, his parents suggested that this should not occur without the courtesy of meeting with and informing the minister of the church he had been a part of since early childhood. Paul looked forward to the encounter, imagining how he might share the joys of this new found faith with his minister, subtly suggesting that he had never found this in the Presbyterian church. The minister was a wise and godly man. Paul cherishes the memory of Rev. John Hawkridge to this day. After Paul telling him in rather arrogant terms why it was time for him to move to a more vibrant church, Rev. Hawkridge graciously conceded that this might be for Paul's good and released him to pursue his faith. After this phase of the conversation was over the subject changed to Paul's terminally ill Aunt Helen. Rev. Hawkridge suggested that Paul could use his new found faith in praying for his very ill aunt. Paul's response was typical of the fervent theology that he had recently been exposed to. He explained that he would pray and that, of course, God would heal his aunt. John Hawkridge quietly nodded his head and, much to Paul's surprise, stated that he too had no doubt that God would heal Aunt Helen. But then came the all-important conditioning words: "Even if He chooses to do so in the resurrection."

These words have conditioned our lives for the past three decades. New perspective dawned and the liberty of having eternity placed consciously within our hearts began to impact the way in which we handled the challenges that came our way. The fact is that we are not temporal or time-bound people waiting for eternity to finally come some day. We are eternal beings living within the restriction of time and space. This helps cast a different light on the vagaries of life. It prevents us superficially "cursing" the darkness, but rather determining to find a spark of hope that will dispel it. We have discovered that we were actually created to cope with pain and, yes, even grief. What we were not created for was to harbour resentment and consistent regret.

Theologically this is called eschatological hope. Not some far away, desperate hope to be taken out of the dark world in which we live, but a confident, humble reassurance that we can walk in the light in the midst of darkness, suffering or sadness. It does not take the pain away every time, but creates a wonderful capacity to wipe away tears, turn sorrow into joy and rejoice in the midst of sorrow. We mourn, but not as those without hope. We have this overwhelming reassurance that He who begins a good work in us will complete it. The timing is God's, the grace is ours.

In the summer of 2007 Paul was diagnosed with a very dangerously dilated aortic aneurism. It involved very intricate and complicated surgery for which fifteen hours was scheduled. (Much more on this subject later). We felt the emotion, the edge of fear and the concern that something of this gravity places upon people. But, looking back, we also enjoyed remarkable levels of assurance, comfort and the care of an amazing God who we loved throughout. There was no need to ask angry questions or have resentful responses. We lived with the reassurance that He makes everything beautiful in His time – even if His time is the resurrection.

To our many friends who have to deal with pain and grief we say with a certain confidence that one day all tears will be wiped away and all hurt relieved. Until that day there is the hope of eternity within our hearts, the sure knowledge that God's grace will see us through and sustain us. For those that are sick there is the hope of divine healing, the miraculous, the supernatural, but there is equally the prospect of an eternity where the radiant face of Christ shines and those who know Him look up with grateful hearts, knowing that whatever life threw at us, it was worth it all.

Endnotes

24. For a good introduction to issues in the early Church see: J. H. Kane, *A Concise History of the Christian World Mission: A Panoramic View of Missions from Pentecost to the Present* (Grand Rapids: Baker Academic, 1978). This is a helpful book in gaining an overview of the expansion of Christianity over two thousand years.
25. See A. M. Renwick and A.M Harman, *The Story of the Church* (Downers Grove: InterVarsity Press, third edition, 2004).
26. D. MacCulloch, *The Reformation: A History* (New York: Penguin Group, 2003).
27. A helpful book in this regard is B. J. Walsh & S. C. Keesmaat, *Colossians Remixed: Subverting the Empire* (Downers Grove, IL: InterVarsity Press, 2004)

Just a Little Knife

*Learning to trust in the
smallest of things*

"God will never, never, never let us down if we have faith and
put our trust in Him. He will always look after us. So we must
cleave to Jesus. Our whole life must simply be woven
into Jesus."
—Mother Teresa

*"But I trust in you, O LORD; I say, 'You are my God.
My times are in your hands.'"*
(Psalm 31:14-15)

Christians believe that the Bible is one of the primary ways in
which God has communicated His will and way to human
beings. It describes the interaction between God and man from
the earliest of times and gives insight into what we can expect
at the end of time.

However, it is not really quite as simple as that. The Bible
was composed by different people over hundreds of years. It
was written in different languages and has subsequently been
translated into thousands more. It has two parts – the Old and
New Testaments.[28] These two parts were written in different
contexts with a vast array of different global forces involved.
There were different empires and rulers, philosophers and

priests and customs and practices involved during the writing of the different parts of the Bible. Some parts of the Bible are history and record in big brush strokes how God has dealt with different people groups. Other parts are poetic with all the nuances of the artists' souls expressed. Every part is written by men inspired by God.[29] There is no part that was delivered by angels or which simply fell from the sky.

This makes the Bible a unique collection of writings bound together by an eternal perspective of the eternal God, who has stated very clearly that He wants to enjoy a relationship with humankind. However, the real issue is not whether we believe that the Bible is God's Word to us, but rather how we interpret this truth. The Bible is not a mantra that should be repeated over and over again. It is not a collection of words that must be individually expounded. It is a vast, panoramic view of the way in which God deals with us. It shows the consistent principles of God's interaction with people.[30]

One of the first principles in learning how to interpret the Bible is to understand the concept of progressive revelation. In other words, over hundreds of years God progressively revealed His character and will enabling us to know Him and serve Him better. Ultimately God reveals Himself to us in the person and work of Jesus Christ, whose teachings bring to a climax all the other things collated in the Bible. We know the will, character and ways of God much better by understanding the whole of the Bible, placing each part carefully into its rightful context and then seeing it through the life and teachings of Christ.

Possibly the single most recurring theme in the Bible about how God relates to us is *faith*. Biblical faith has many dimensions to it, but must always be grounded in the biblical concept. In other words, it can never be some contemporary form of self-help or even positive thinking. Its primary component is *obedience*. Abraham is called the Father of faith and his chief characteristic was not what he accomplished or the wealth that he had, but his complete obedience.[31] Put another way, faith does not really have much to do with what we can get from God; rather it has much more to do with what we can give to God. Only then can it become the *"substance of things hoped for and the evidence of things not seen."*[32]

We sometimes refer to faith theologically in terms of creative purpose. In other words, one of the primary instincts within the human heart is to reach out beyond ourselves and trust. It is only the bitter and the burnt who refuse to trust or live with hope. Babies trust almost completely. It is only as their trust is disappointed through poor parenting, irresponsible teasing or the denial of necessary provision that they start to harden and lose trust. Trust that is disappointed can make children bitter by their early teens. This is true for everyone and pertains to the spiritual realm as well. A cold, stoic belief in God without the vibrant expectation of hope will result in an introverted religion that has nothing at all attractive to it. God delights in us expressing our obedience to Him. One of the best ways of starting this journey is to have a heart full of hope, a deep confidence that trust will not be misplaced and that faith in God will be rewarded. This principle is reinforced throughout the Bible. Jesus summarises it by stating that if we have faith for little God will trust us with much.

We learnt this lesson at a relatively early stage. Soon after we were married we found ourselves on an amazing journey of faith that would eventually take us to twenty-three different nations in about a two-year period. We were in our early twenties and had embarked on a radical adventure during which we honestly believed God would open doors, enable us to minister in churches, youth groups and schools and provide all of our financial needs. In many ways, this trip cast the die for much of our future as we have endeavoured to initiate new things and serve God faithfully. It was, however, a little radical as we literally trusted God to lead us and provide for us on a daily basis.

We had received some kind invitations to speak in a number of churches in Pennsylvania, USA. To each we responded enthusiastically and enjoyed a time of sharing in some great faith communities in the eastern part of that State. By this time we had accumulated just enough money through the kindness of these churches to buy an old car. It was a huge gas-guzzler but proved reliable and got us where we needed to go. In order to stretch our meagre resources as far as possible we would often buy a little bread and cheese and eat whilst travelling between destinations. Carol had been raised in a respectable household and breaking great hunks of bread off and passing them to Paul with a piece of cheese seemed a little uncouth! One day she asked whether we should ask God to provide a knife. Paul appreciated her naivety and simple trust, but thought that this was going too far. We were poor but not that poor! A little knife would be easy to purchase. Not wanting to dampen Carol's enthusiastic faith he suggested that she go ahead and ask God, really not believing for a moment that this kind of prayer would interest Him. In the simple way that pure-hearted Christ-followers express themselves to God, Carol simply informed God of our situation, mentioned how she did not enjoy breaking the bread into pieces and said how nice it would be to have a little knife to do the job.

That night a kind and generous older couple hosted us. We have not kept in contact so we do not even recall their names. But we will never forget their hospitality. They had faced several family traumas and seemed to find the company of an enthusiastic and innocent young couple restorative. We spoke into the early hours of the morning before retiring to bed. Typically there was a large breakfast waiting for us the next morning. We had learnt to enjoy these meals, not knowing when the next one would come!

We finally said our goodbyes and packed our meagre belongings into the cavernous boot of the car. Waving out of both front windows we drove down the driveway on our way to the next speaking engagement. As Paul checked the rear-view mirror he suddenly noticed the gentleman running towards us beckoning us to stop. We halted as he came up out of breath. He quickly informed us that he had clearly felt God speak to him as we left and would we just wait exactly where we were for a few minutes. He disappeared into the house and then came out again a few minutes later with some objects in his hands. He was glowing with joy as he handed us two sets of camping cutlery – the kind where the knife, fork and spoon are all clipped together. He said again that he was certain God had told him to give these to us. We were amazed, expressed our thanks and left that driveway feeling quite overwhelmed at the specific kindness and caring love of our heavenly Father.

Over the months that followed we experienced a number of similar events. On one occasion we were finding the Pennsylvania winter colder than we had expected. Carol again prayed for God to provide for us. This time it was a pair of gloves that was requested. Less than twenty-four hours later we were preaching in another little church and were ushered into the pastor's office before the service began. On his desk were two small parcels with a simple label on each: "From Jesus". When we opened them we found a pair of gloves each and a beautiful scarf each. More than we had asked for!

Remarkably, in each of these instances and many besides, there was no way for the donors to have any idea what we had asked God for. We were convinced from an early age that God does care for His children and desires to show His love and provision in very specific ways. The Bible encourages us to pray and make our requests known to God. Central to the whole concept of New Testament Christianity is that God has come close to us and made Himself known to us. One way in which He does this is through acts of kindness and gracious provision. Of course, God is never to be thought of as some endless source who responds to our every whim and fancy. He is not a celestial Santa Claus and does not always provide all that we want.[33] But He is our heavenly Father, He does care, He is intimately involved in the lives of those who follow Him through Christ.

We have discovered that the teaching of Jesus is true. We learned to simply trust God for the needs that we had and that has not changed over the past three decades and more. We still express our trust in God. We still hold hands across the meal table and give thanks for His provision and anticipate His continued supply. Is this just naïve? We think not. It represents the discipline of living grateful lives that are not tainted with presumption or arrogant faith claims. It is the natural result of a theology that confidently believes in a loving and caring God who involves Himself in the lives of His children. We understand that a life of obedience that sincerely endeavours to serve and follow God and obey His leading will result in the kind response of God in provision, even at the most basic level.

To our readers we present this challenge: trust God. Try to work through the multi-layered propaganda of contemporary Church which has become overly obsessed with material things. Understand the fact that we live this side of eternity with the harsh realities of sustaining life. The need might be only a little knife, but the principle is much bigger. God is near, He is loving and kind and He looks for people who will live in simple obedience making Him their priority. The response from God will always be acts of gracious kindness and provision.

Endnotes

28. D.G. Fee and D. Stuart, *How to Read the Bible For all its Worth: A Guide to Understanding the Bible* (Grand Rapids: Zondervan, 1993). See also D.G. Fee and D. Stuart, *How to Read the Bible Book by Book: A Guided Tour* (Grand Rapids: Zondervan, 2002). These two books are helpful in establishing good Bible reading patterns and understanding the whole message of the Bible.
29. 2 Timothy 3:16
30. E. Dyck (Ed.) *The Act of Reading the Bible: A Multi-Disciplinary Approach to Biblical Interpretation* (Downers Grove: InterVarsity Press, 1996). This book should help those who would like to expand their ability in understanding and interpreting the Bible.
31. Genesis 12
32. Hebrews 11:1
33. M. Volf, *Free of Charge: Giving and Forgiving in a Culture Stripped of Grace* (Grand Rapids, MI:, Zondervan, 2005) , p27 states, "...many people think of God ... as a Santa Claus conveniently enlarged to divine proportions ... A Santa Claus demands nothing from us. A divine Santa is the indiscriminately giving and inexhaustibly fertile source of everything that is, and everything that is to come our way. God is an inexhaustibly fertile source of everything."

Times and Seasons

Maximising opportunities –
the grace of patience

"God allows us to experience the low points of life in order to
teach us lessons that we could learn in no other way."
C.S. Lewis

"He has made everything beautiful in its time."
(Ecclesiastes 3:11)

One of the characteristics of the frenetic lifestyles so many of
us live is the need to order everything according to a specific
time. We have sophisticated software that reminds us of everything that is scheduled and our lives become calibrated by small
time slots into which we seem to cram almost impossible
commitments.

It is tempting to think that human beings always lived this
way, but this is not the case. The combined effects of technology
and the thinking produced by the Enlightenment have
changed the way in which we live our lives.[34] We move in very
personal spheres with limited dependency either on our family
or a wide circle of friends, and thus life often passes in a blur
with one month melting into another seamlessly. If it were not
for the obvious weather changes we would hardly know that
the year was progressing as we turn each day into another
struggle to fulfil obligations, finish critical tasks and cram in

just a little bit of entertainment along the way. We view thousands of images in a single day, have high-tech equipment in most rooms of our houses and work places, and wonder why we sometimes feel just a little weary!

We can do very little about changing the pace of our world, but we can change the way we live in it. This is especially true when it comes to developing our theology. Put another way, the understanding that we have about God and His ways will make a big difference to the way in which we evaluate our experiences of life. Instead of everything being time-critical, where we push for specific outcomes and instant results, we can develop a grace of patience. God is not time-bound and it is this interface between our time-space realm and the eternal realm that creates many issues in the lives of Christ-followers.

This conflict between our world and the world that God inhabits can cause confusion about our perceived answers to prayer. We have been conditioned to getting quick results and when our prayers are not answered in the way and at the time we think appropriate, we somehow question God, expecting Him to conform to our image rather than resting in the sure knowledge that He will do all things well in His time.[35] This can seem so defeatist, but it is not really. It is a high expression of faith to declare our trust in God and then to retain a sweet, happy disposition while He works things out in His way. We wish we had more answers, we wish we could explain every unanswered prayer but, looking back over many years, we are as sure today as ever: God knows best and His answers sometimes are worked out over times and seasons, not months, days or hours.[36]

Another area of conflict that we have observed is in regard to the way in which God uses us in our different seasons of life. Parenting is a typical example. With the benefit of hindsight (and grown children) we are amazed that we survived the parenting adventure! Life has no dress rehearsals and we cannot be sure that anyone is really prepared for parenting. There are countless good books (which are a help) and hopefully there is an extended family that can support as well. But, in the final analysis, parenting is a rough ride, filled with immensely happy experiences, which we take without ever having gone that way before. The theological principle to grasp is that life is more a progression of seasons than a desperate bid to last until the summer holidays or get through until the Spring break.

Like seasons, life has a vast array of colours, temperatures, smells and feelings. None are to be resisted or regretted; all are to be maximised to their full potential. We have discovered that there is such a thing as the winter of the soul. At one point Paul recalls a six-month period during which there seemed to be a dark shadow cast across his life. Prayer had little meaning and all sense of joy and fulfilment were gone. To this day we have no idea what caused this. We know that it was not the result of wrongdoing. We also know that throughout this period there was constant dialogue between us, trying to discover why Paul felt that way. There were no feelings of bitterness being harboured that could atrophy the soul, as appeared to be happening. We went through the routine of enquiring if there was unforgiveness in some deep recess of Paul's soul. We even considered the possibility that this was some form of depression. We found no answer as each of these little investigations led nowhere. Then, like a refreshing storm, the springtime came again. It was actually immediately following this long, dark season that the vision for Africa School of Missions was birthed. The whole experience of spiritual struggle passed rapidly, life came, the prison gates burst open and a season of amazing fruitfulness followed. Winter will always turn to springtime. Sometimes grace grows best in winter and the flowers of spring are all the more beautiful.

When Anna was just eighteen months old and Jason a few days old Paul was required to leave the family in order to fulfil his national service obligation. He was able to serve as a chaplain, but this did not dull the pain and uncertainty of long periods of separation. Since leaving Bible College we had served side by side and Carol had always been as involved in ministry as Paul had. Now her world collapsed into the confines of single parenting. This was a season we were not well prepared to face. There were the obvious feelings of loneliness, at times almost desperation as Carol raised two tiny children on her own. There were the financial struggles with very little by way of salary coming into the home. But, what was most challenging was the relative absence of ministry. Carol felt a sense of detachment in our own church. Of course, people were as supportive as they could be. We were not really alone, but it certainly felt that way. Paul felt helpless as he was marched around a parade ground completing basic training. Carol felt cut off as she cared for her precious little ones, but felt the pain of being limited in what she could do in terms of ministry.

There were brief moments of respite over the next eighteen months. However, this time was incredibly stretching and, at times, very uncertain. There was a time when Paul was posted to a remote army camp on the northern Namibian border and communication between us was almost non-existent.

Some years later we moved and it was during the relocation that we discovered that each of us had kept the letters we had written to each other during this difficult time. Paul had numbered each letter, so it was easy to put them into chronological order. Carol filed each one and we had the opportunity to look back over the season that we had gone through by reading through the letters. What an enriching experience this proved to be! There were the obvious phrases expressing loneliness. There were whole paragraphs in which we expressed our love and affection for each other. But then there were all the references to the goodness of God and the grace that He was giving to get us through the time of separation and uncertainty. The language was rich and written so spontaneously that there was no way for it to be some superficial expression of religious hope. It was a confident expression of trust in a God who knows the end from the beginning. The correspondence is a marvellous chronicle of the goodness of a kind God who will never test us beyond that which we are able to bear.

Today those letters also give us some wonderful insight into the growth and development of our children during that time. Carol records each little phase in faithful detail in order that Paul could share the moment. The first crawl, the first smile and the first word spoken by Jason are all there for us to recall and celebrate. Looking back it was a rich season. It was stretching, lonely and, at times, even confusing. But God was there and He grew capacities within each of us that have served us well until this day.

Carol recalls a special moment during this time. Paul had received the news that, after many weeks of basic training, a family visit was allowed. With typical military protocol the officers informed him that his immediate family could visit, but there were certain conditions. Firstly, he had to stand for an inspection in which every crease in his trousers would be scrutinised to make sure that they were perfect. Then, when the family arrived, he was not allowed to lose his military dignity by running forward and hugging them. Rather, he was to walk forward in a dignified way, pause appropriately and salute them! Thereafter he could make physical contact (only briefly!) and spend about an hour of precious time together. He was allowed one phone call to explain all of this.

Carol was perplexed. She had no desire to meet her husband and have him salute her. She wanted a hug, a kiss and a special moment in his arms. The day for this special meeting dawned. Carol put the children in the car and began the journey towards the military base. Anna was only twenty months, but seemed to understand how unique this day was. Carol parked the car and approached the parade ground. Eagle-eyed corporals were positioned around the ground to ensure that there was no breaking of protocol or soppy expressions of sentimentality. With butterflies in his tummy Paul scanned the cars as they arrived and then waited anxiously for the family to make their way to the rendezvous point. What a special moment!

When Carol arrived with Anna walking beside her clutching her hand and Jason in her arms, they followed the signs to the point where they would wait for Paul to step forward, salute and then greet them. It was then that all the careful military planning failed completely. At a distance little Anna recognised her Dad. She spontaneously let go of her mother's hand and ran as fast as her little legs could carry her past the corporals (and every other officer for that matter) and with complete abandon threw herself into her Dad's arms. There was no time for a salute, no time for protocol as a dad and his little girl were reunited. To be honest, it melted most hearts around the parade ground that day. The separation was instantly forgotten, the lonely nights seemed to melt away and we were all reminded that tough seasons come to an end and difficult times pass.

This is completely consistent with the Bible message. We are reminded that weeping endures for a night, but joy comes in the morning. The lovely, poetic language of the Psalms tells us that God will bring forth the justice of our cause like the noon-day sun. In other words, the correct management of our souls during seasons that are dry, dark or uncertain will result in the passing of that season into a time of joy and celebration.

There are some principles that are important to learn about

this soul management during tough seasons. Firstly, it is important not to try to artificially shorten the season. As tempting as it might seem to escape the difficult time we are facing, it is important to ask God for grace, find some supportive friends and allow the season to pass. God makes things beautiful in His time and we can sometimes make inappropriate decisions that restrict the long-term benefit God intends for us by allowing a difficult season in the first place. Then, it is so important to guard our hearts during tough seasons. It is easy to take on the mentality of a victim and to seek attention or sympathy. This, too, will diminish the long term benefit of coming through difficult times to the dawn of a new season. We constantly urge our friends who are going through confusing or even hurtful times to avoid making big decisions or rash choices. Let God's grace be enough for each day and His strength enough for each part of the journey. The season will pass! The sun will shine again![37]

Endnotes

34. For insight into the transitioning eras from Enlightenment to Postmodernism see D. J. Bosch, *Transforming Mission: Paradigm Shifts in Theology of Mission* (Maryknoll, NY: Orbis, 1991). See also pp3-4 where Bosch discusses some of the features of the era we currently find ourselves in. See also P. Tickle, *The Great Emergence: How Christianity is Changing and Why* (Grand Rapids, MI: Baker Books, 2009). Her book highlights five major transitional moves in the past 2000 years.
35. Ecclesiastes 3:11
36. D. Willard, *Knowing Christ Today: Why We Can Trust Spiritual Knowledge* (New York, NY: HarperCollins Publishers, 2009), pp13-34.
37. Tom Wright, *Simply Christian* (London: SPCK, 2006) p33: "One of the central elements of the Christian story is the claim that the paradox of laughter and tears, woven as it is deep into the heart of all human experience, is woven also deep into the heart of God."

Do Not Ripen Too Soon

Pacing ourselves for the long haul

"Every happening, great and small, is a parable whereby God speaks to us, and the art of life is to get the message."
—Malcolm Muggeridge

"Experience: that most brutal of teachers. But you learn, my God you learn."
—C.S. Lewis

"All the days ordained for me were written in your book before one of them came to be."
(Psalm 139:16)

There are some lessons in life that you learn through offence. The key, of course, is managing the offence effectively and working through to the most productive and positive outcome. Offensive statements really should not break or hurt us – they should serve to develop an inner resolve to either correct what has been addressed or to analyse the words and, if they are untrue, to quietly ignore them.

The maxim "Do not ripen too soon" came into our lives in a way that we felt was somewhat offensive. We were always rather energetic about life. From the start of our journey as Christ-followers it seemed only natural to seize whatever opportunity came our way. Although this was spontaneous, we never stopped to think what the long term cost might be to us for taking leadership risks and following our visionary hearts. For most of the time this zealous approach to life worked. We gladly served wherever opportunity arose and found ourselves in levels of Christian leadership that were, in some ways, beyond our experience and our years.

By the mid-eighties we were involved in the biggest adventure of our lives. Through remarkable circumstances we were leading a missionary training college called Africa School of Missions in the beautiful Mpumalanga province of South Africa. We had a fifty-acre campus with significant buildings and before long people were travelling to us from all over the world to be trained as missionaries. We were pioneering new strategies for mission and soon found ourselves speaking in different parts of the world. It was a rapid rise in terms of profile and exposure to the wider Church. We had two young children, were leading a college with over two hundred people resident on the campus and found ourselves engaged in strategic mission events on different continents – and we were only twenty-eight years of age!

It was about this time that Paul spent a morning with an older missionary whom he had grown to love and respect. His name was David Newington and over dozens of years he and his wife had led a literature evangelism ministry called Emmanuel Press. David was a somewhat eccentric English missionary, but if you listened carefully he had a marvellous way of throwing in priceless little gems of wisdom from time to time. Paul loved spending time with him, but on this particular occasion David did offend him. While Paul was excitedly telling him about the latest bit of visionary adventure he was experiencing, David leant back in his chair and without any warning told Paul in no uncertain terms, "Do not ripen too soon." It seemed so inappropriate! This seemed to be a great opportunity for him to encourage a young man. Wasn't this the kind of mentoring moment that older leaders looked for? He seemed to waste it with such an unnecessary warning. What could he have meant?

For Paul, the offence was in what was implied. David's words seemed to suggest that he was running ahead of himself and should take time to be more reflective about life and leadership. It seemed apparent that David was not quite as impressed with our achievements as we thought he ought to be. He was clearly suggesting that we pace ourselves better and take more time to savour the season we were in, rather than be continually pushing forward with the next plan and another visionary project. It was this apparent discouragement that was so offensive. Paul left David's office that day unsure if he ever wanted to go back.

Of course, David was right! He had the perspective that only years and experience can give and, rather than discouraging a young man, he was imparting profound wisdom – wisdom that is sometimes hard to apply during the rapid pace of life in the digital world we all share. David was making it very clear that life is not successful just because it has one or two apparent success stories. What makes life really worth living is developing the ability to celebrate the moment whilst developing stamina for the long haul.

We began to process what we had heard and slowly started learning the need for resilience. This is that amazing life skill and internal discipline that allows you to handle both success and failure well. The one does not cause arrogance and the other does not produce despair. They all become part of the greater, successful whole. We appreciated that the best fruit is that which remains on the branch for the longest possible time. It ripens slowly, drawing the warmth of the sun's rays and resolutely refusing to let go when the storm comes. The longer the ripening process, the sweeter the fruit. This principle for life solidly became a part of our value system and thinking and has served us well ever since.

The principle of not ripening too soon is found again and again in the Bible. Joseph found that life rose to meet him as a young man and he soon became especially loved by his father.[38] It took a pit and prison before he had the resilience to lead a nation through a dramatic economic recovery plan that is still acknowledged by economists. David killed a giant, but God refused to allow him to ripen to soon.[39] Rather, he spent several years as an outlaw learning to lead the most difficult of people before he became the head of government and wisely led his people and established a surplus in the trading account for his nation. Jesus held His own with the scholars of His day by the time he was twelve.[40] Yet, it was only after eighteen years of routine carpentry work that He came to prominence and literally changed the course of history.

Of course, the principle of ripening too soon does not imply that people should not seize the moment or the opportunities that come their way. The Bible illustrates instances where God put people like Moses and Joseph through long wilderness experiences.[41] However, there are also instances in the Bible where we are called to *"make the most of every opportunity."*[42] It is this delicate balance of seizing the opportunities that come our way, mingled with the ability to reflect on where we have come from and where we are heading that is vital for Christian maturity. It is also allowing the gracious hand of a loving God to work in our lives to make us fit for His service, and in so doing to ripen and mature into all that He has for us.[43] That is what the psalmist is talking about in Psalm one where he says that a righteous person is like *"a tree planted by streams of water, which yields its fruit in season and whose leaf does not wither."*[44]

We would encourage you to gain a deeper perspective of Christian life, especially if you are enjoying those happy (and at times challenging!) years of early adulthood.[45] Seize opportunities, but understand that it is most important to maximise the current season of life. Please do not wish your life away or only live for the next big event. Resilience is an amazing life skill. It will temper you and make you strong. Stay where you are for the optimum period of time. Avoid rapid decision-making processes and knee-jerk responses to circumstances. Stay on the branch in terms of friendships, faith and responsibilities. None of these massive areas of life are worth fracturing for an ill-considered decision or an impulsive move. Simply, don't ripen too soon.[46]

Endnotes

38. Genesis chapters 37-50
39. 1 Samuel 17
40. Luke 2:41-52
41. Exodus 2 & 3, Genesis 37-41. M. Volf, *Exclusion & Embrace: A Theological Exploration of Identity, Otherness and Reconciliation* (Nashville, TN: Abingdon Pres, 1996). Out of the suffering and horror of his people in the Balkans, this is a testimony to the profound hope of the Gospel in the midst of human conflict and pain.
42. Ephesians 5:16, Galatians 6:10 and Colossians 4:5
43. Ephesians 4:12, Philippians 1:6, 2 Corinthians 4:7
44. Psalm 1:3
45. Willard, *Knowing Christ Today*. In this book Willard explains how important it is to live out our faith in a secular age.
46. O. Guinness, *The Call: Finding and Fulfilling the Central Purpose of your Life* (Nashville, Tennessee: Word Publishing, 1998). Any of Os Guinness' books are worth the read.

Mainly For, Seldom Against

The grace of tolerance

"The responsibility of tolerance lies with those who have the wider vision."
—George Eliot

"Therefore in the present case I advise you: Leave these men alone! Let them go! For if their purpose is of human origin, it will fail. But if it is from God, you will not be able to stop these men; you will only find yourselves fighting against God."
(Acts 5:38-39)

Generalisations can be dangerous. This is especially true when it comes to theological issues. We have to remember that the expression of the Church that we see in the 21st Century is the result of thousands of years of spiritual journeying through multiple cultures and many nations. Faith has served different purposes at different times. For some it was a lifeline to a better life in the hereafter, especially during times of plague when thousands were dying. For others, such as the early Pilgrims who sailed to America, it was the hope of freedom and the building of a functioning society without fear or prejudice.

In more recent times faith has been expressed in other ways. For example, in the late 1950s and through the 1960s faith became a symbol of liberation for many in Latin America.

After years of dictatorship, the grassroots members of churches rose up and used their faith as part of their reason for inciting liberation movements that were, ironically, Marxist in their political thought. Many churches and church leaders throughout the South American continent adopted a whole new theological position called Liberation Theology.

In a similar way there was a theological reaction to the demise of colonialism in Africa. African Americans shared the pain of their brothers and sisters across Africa who were trying to throw off the restraints of colonial rule. Black Theology was the result, in which the vestiges of white European-centric theology were challenged and, where possible, eradicated. Jesus was stripped of His traditionally Western lily white complexion and "Africanised" in an attempt to keep the central features of Christian faith without their cultural baggage.[47] This theological process helped spawn a massive movement of churches called the "African Indigenous Church Movement" which now has many millions of adherents. To many, their theology is suspect, containing what missiologists call syncretism.[48] In other words, there is a perceived blend of Christian thought and practice with old tribal ways and their accompanying animist beliefs.

In the West there have been many similar expressions of Christianity that seem to be equal part culture and equal part Christian.[49] As America experienced economic boom times in the 1960s, churches and their leaders began to combine the national aspiration for wealth and prosperity with a theological argument that accommodated this. For centuries we have developed liturgies that include prayer for the Sovereign and for the country. During the awful wars that wracked Europe in the 20th Century there were military chaplains on both sides, equally as sincere, praying that God would give their troops the victory over the others. For most of the rest of the world it was terribly confusing seeing so called Christian nations warring with one another. Most recently there has been a rapid multiplication of Christian media. Some books are completely fictitious, but can be read as though they are doctrine. Music and song styles are as much cultural as they are spiritual.

So where does this leave the earnest Christ-follower who really wants to serve God faithfully and discover first century Christianity? Firstly, it is really important to remind ourselves that the New Testament Church was far from perfect.[50] It was filled with division and records the fact that there were difficult people doing their best to make things hard for people like the apostle Paul. We also know there were moral issues and that there were many struggles within the Church on how true faith was to be maintained within the cultural forms of the different people groups that were being reached for Christ. The Gospel in culture is not something new – it has been a part of the landscape of the Church since the earliest of times. In fact, the first great council of the Church called in Jerusalem centred almost entirely on how to accommodate cultural forms whilst not contaminating true faith.[51]

Secondly, we can go even further back and note that God seemed to tolerate culture within the worship expressions that He allowed. As long as we need food, furniture, education, families and business we will have cultural expression. When Solomon built the temple in Jerusalem there were twelve bronze bulls supporting the laver.[52] These bulls had more of an association with pagan worship than the worship of God, but somehow God's glory still fell on the temple. Throughout His dealings with human beings God seems to be much more tolerant with our time-bound perspective on things than we are. Throughout history true faith has prevailed through multiple cultural expressions.[53]

As human beings seek to relate to their understanding of who God is and how to serve Him, God has allowed multiple expressions of worship. Even as Christianity was spreading its wings for the first time there were some within the Jewish hierarchy who dared to believe that this might be a genuine continuation of God's revelation.[54] For example Gamaliel, the Jewish scholar and leader who strongly advocated that the new expression of faith surrounding the life and death of the humble Galilean called Jesus should not be persecuted but allowed to develop. He based his argument on the incredibly liberating thought that what is of God will last and what is not will soon disappear.[55]

As the Church takes on various forms and shapes, this tolerance is equally liberating today. We were never created to be watchdogs over God's work – the Holy Spirit is more than able to take care of His work. It is not for us to take to our pulpits and be constantly comparing one church with another and then declaring why one is clearly better than the other. Does this mean that we are to accept just anything? Of course not. It simply means that we do not become consumed by every new initiative, every new form of worship, and the church down the road that seems to have so much wrong with it yet still attracts people. It means that we become committed to a simple and humble faith that always seeks to honour God and we celebrate the diversity that exists in the wider Body of Christ. Jesus reminded His disciples that it was only in the final judgment that God separates the wheat from the weeds, so it seems wise not to obsessively oppose things when we can celebrate the many good and wholesome things that God is doing. We cannot be friends with everyone, but we can determine to be enemies with no one.

This is the grace of tolerance and it is a vital component of the certain life. The apostle Paul came to a place of such internal liberty that he stated that even if people were preaching from wrong motives or to create problems, he would rejoice that Christ was being preached anyway. This echoes Jesus' own teaching in Luke 9: 50 where He told John not to prevent people from casting out demons in His name because, *"whoever is not against you is for you."* In other words, a tolerant grace is learning to accept diversity and to withhold criticism when people seek to honour the name of Christ – even when their methods are somewhat questionable or their message does not conform to every detail of doctrine we hold dear.

We learnt this lesson at a very formative stage of our Christian leadership. We were associate pastors in a great church that had enjoyed a number of years of consistent growth. We found ourselves in a vibrant and happy faith community, enjoying seeing God do many wonderful things in people's lives. At about the same time that we began our ministry in this great church, another church started up a few miles away. The pastor of this new church was something of a celebrity who had gained the support of a group of churches in America, giving him the opportunity to launch a new church with significant resources and profile. The church grew rapidly, but it seemed as though there was an imbalance in terms of the message being preached. There was certainly no comprehensive theology or an attempt to try to moderate a very strong emphasis on the health, wealth and prosperity message.

Our senior pastor became very distressed. He did his home-work, checked what was being preached in this new church and then started a campaign to discredit this church and the message being proclaimed there. We hold our former pastor in great respect to this day and must state that he always sought to show the fault in the message, not in the man who was preaching it. However, the whole thing became almost obsessive. Each Sunday morning there was another sermon on why the message at the other church was wrong. Carefully crafted Bible studies exposed the error adopted by the church down the road. This went on for weeks and eventually months.

Some intriguing things began to happen. Firstly, it seemed as though growth in our church plateauxed and the real sense of vibrant joy that had been there before was not quite so evident. Then, some of our members began to wonder why so much attention was being given to the other church and decided to go there and investigate for themselves. They did not find things as bad as they had expected and some decided to relocate and join the new church. This was all very dismaying to our pastor who really thought he was defending God's good name and establishing true doctrine. How could people be so easily led astray?

At about the same time Paul was involved in trying to resolve some issues surrounding church politics and became caught up in a number of controversies. He will never forget the day when an older minister took him aside, placed his arms around his shoulders and said, "Remember, if the spirit is wrong, everything is wrong." By this he meant that, even if the cause is right, if it is fought with a bitter or angry spirit it makes the whole thing wrong. We slowly began to realise that it is best to develop the grace of tolerance, knowing that it is God who *"brings forth the justice of our cause like the noonday sun."* He is fully capable of taking care of His work and His people without us constantly taking sides or obsessively defending our position. Thus, a formative lesson in developing certain lives was to be mainly *for* things and seldom *against*. We have maintained our principles, we do not bend on morals, but we seek to rejoice with those who rejoice and mourn with those who mourn. Put another way, we desire to see the best, love always and let time tell whether something is of God or not.

To those who are leaders reading this we suggest the development of a quiet resolve to avoid becoming cynical or even bitter at the actions of others. A quiet reassurance that God is in control of His Church and that we should thus simply get on with what He has entrusted to us is very liberating. To those who are taking the early steps of being Christ-followers we would urge that you test things, check the credentials of the people who are influencing you for Christ and then walk forward in your faith with grace and caution.

A certain life believes the best, seeks to champion all who desire to do something for God and avoids becoming a negative watchdog of the faith, contending for minor points of doctrine, whilst there are thousands of people who need our love and Christian commitment.

Endnotes

47. To gain helpful insight to this process see L. Sanneh, *Whose Religion is Christianity? The Gospel Beyond the West* (Grand Rapids: Eerdmans, 2003).
48. See A. F. Walls, *The Missionary Movement in Christian History: Studies in the Transmission of Faith* (Maryknoll: Orbis Books, 2005), pp111-178.
49. G. Boyd, *The Myth of a Christian Nation: How the Quest for Political Power is Destroying the Church* (Grand Rapids, MI: Zondervan, 2005), deals with this particular concern.
50. See 1 Corinthians 1:10-17
51. Acts 15
52. Jeremiah 52:20
53. Walls, *The Missionary Movement*, pp43-54
54. P. Jenkins, *The Next Christendom: the Coming of Global Christianity* (Oxford: Oxford University press, 2002).
55. Acts 5:38-39

Defining Moments

Obeying God's call

"He is no fool who gives what he cannot keep to gain what he cannot lose."
—Jim Elliott

"God is God. Because He is God, He is worthy of my trust and obedience. I will find rest nowhere but in His holy will, a will that is unspeakably beyond my largest notions of what He is up to."
—Elisabeth Elliott

"Speak, Lord, for your servant is listening."
(1 Samuel 3: 9)

An evaluation of any life that has been lived certainly – that is with meaning, direction and influence – will inevitably reveal some or other defining experience or moment. In the Bible this is certainly true. Moses' life was dramatically changed through his encounter with God at the burning bush.[56] Joshua had his defining leadership encounter at Jericho and this established his leadership for many years.[57] Gideon met the Angel of the Lord whilst threshing in a wine press for fear of being discovered.[58] This transformed him into a leader who would lead an entire nation into liberty. David had his encounter with Goliath and so on.[59]

This is not only a biblical principle but a human reality. Even a cursory reading of history will reveal how people of significant influence went through either one or a series of defining moments and experiences which resulted in a determination or an opportunity that changed their entire future.

Theologically this concept can be described. It is the interface between the eternal purposes of God, that are not restricted by either time or space, and the time-bound life of people. As these two forces combine in the life of an individual, change, purpose and destiny all begin to find focus and the plans and purposes of God become a reality in our lives. Everyone who has become a truly devoted follower of Jesus Christ should have this theological awareness, that part of our expression of obedience to God is to expect that He can and will reveal Himself to us. This God-revelation forms the foundation of living certainly and not superstitiously or fatalistically. Christians do not accept the worldview that somehow we are victims of a natural law that sets us on an inevitable course of life over which we have no control. Rather, we live with a deep awareness that we can discover the purposes of God and that our own prayerfulness and expectation somehow influences this process.

Possibly one of the most defining of these moments for us was the founding of Africa School of Missions (ASM) in 1985. Although many other narratives recorded in this book occurred prior to this time, we choose to share this story with you now as it is so central to our lives and illustrates how many other aspects of our journey either helped develop our understanding of God's will for us in pioneering this missionary training school, or have continued to help us serve God faithfully to the present day.

By early 1983 we had already jammed huge amounts of

experiences into our young lives. We had ministered in many nations, served as assistant pastors in two large churches and welcomed our two precious children into the world. Additionally, Paul had recently completed a time of mandatory national service as a military chaplain. We were now the senior pastors of our home church on the eastern side of the city of Johannesburg. Fairview Assembly, as it was known, had been a great mother church over the years. There were families who fondly remembered the early days of this church when a tent was pitched on a vacant piece of land and evangelistic services were conducted over several months. There were eyewitnesses to miracles of healing that occurred during that time and many came to Christ. As a result, a vibrant local church was established and a permanent building erected. Over the years many churches were planted out from the mother church and Fairview Assembly had been the source of spiritual life and blessing to thousands.

We, however, were invited to the pastorate after a painful split had occurred and a relatively small group of discouraged people left. Undaunted, we committed to leading the church and soon dozens of young people began attending with many coming to Christ. Within a year the building was filled, we had initiated some major renovations of the facilities, installed a new sound system and were enjoying the obvious favour of God on our ministry.

The church provided us with a lovely home, our children were already booked into some of the best schools in the area and we should have been enjoying an overwhelming sense of fulfilment and satisfaction. In fact, quite the opposite was the case. Paul descended into a deep spiritual crisis. It did not overflow into family or social life and all continued well in the life of the church. However, in private times and those times of spiritual devotion and reflection his heart seemed empty and his life confusing. He did his best to bridle this feeling and ensure that it was not in any way imposed on those he loved or the church that he served. It did, nevertheless continue for six long and confusing months. In reflecting on this time, it was clear to Paul that he was not in crisis regarding his faith in God, nor did he doubt the authenticity of his salvation. It had to do with his sense of God's will for his ministry. Although difficult to articulate at the time, the struggle was regarding the discovery of God's primary purpose for his life and a deep determination to resist the ordinary.

In the July of 1983 the internal crisis within Paul's heart had grown in intensity. He resented the sense of going through the motions regarding his ministry and finally, in a desperate moment in the loneliness of his church office, he cried out asking God to reveal Himself again. What followed was a life-defining moment.

As honestly as Paul can remember he is still not sure whether the next few minutes in his office were spiritual in the sense of a form of vision or physical in the sense that his experience was with his human senses. He recalls his office flaming with light and how he spontaneously dropped to his knees next to his desk. The whole experience was accompanied by a tranquil silence, but instinctively he began to discern God's voice in his heart. In fact, within minutes he knew three things that have, in many ways, defined our lives ever since. The first was that we were to leave pastoral ministry. The second was that we were to impact nations and the third was that we were to trust God on behalf of others. To this day those three statements ring in our hearts.

Sensing the importance of the moment, Paul immediately left his office, drove home and ran into the house. We often smile as we remember him reaching out his hand, taking Carol by the arm and literally pinning her up against a wall. All that he could say was, "Carol, God is moving us into a new dimension of ministry!" Carol was relieved to see some life returning to her husband, who had so obviously been battling an internal crisis over the previous number of months. Instinctively knowing that this was not a passing emotional moment, but rather a significant time of God initiating something new, she responded positively. By this time in our lives possessions had no particular hold on us and so a comfortable house and nice furniture were not an impediment to us following the purpose of God in our lives.

We were starting to learn that not all spiritual experiences are exhilarating and exciting. Because God sees way beyond our limited perspective He does allow times of internal reflection and even crisis. Bit by bit God brilliantly crafts His will into our lives teaching us to trust Him and have confidence that He is working everything together for our good. We grew increasingly aware that God was much more committed to the things He wants to do *in* us than the things He wants to do *through* us. Put another way, God has a greater interest in our character than He has in our actions. Although painful at the time, Paul realised that those long, hard months were a part of God's gracious work, producing a deeper capacity in his life for handling leadership responsibilities.

We remember holding hands in our bedroom and prayerfully expressing our availability to God to follow and serve Him in whatever way He chose. The first two days following this amazing experience were exhilarating. We spoke animatedly about what could be in store for us. We prayed excitedly about our future and asked God to lead us. However, by the third and then the fourth day the feeling of delight began to leave us as nothing further developed. Terrified that he should slip back into the dark embrace of the crisis that had been a part of his life for so long, Paul suggested that we get away for just a day or two, during which time we could pray further regarding what it was that God was leading us into.

At the time we had friends who were part of the staff on a guest farm that was situated about a four-hour journey away from our home. We made arrangements to spend a night with them, packed up our car and, with our two little ones in the back, made our way to our friends' home. Our only outstanding recollection of the brief time there was a deep impression which Carol had late in the evening that God's ways are above our ways, recollecting an ancient Scripture found in the book of Isaiah.[60] It was not long before we were packing up the car again and heading home in time for services at church the next day.

Amazingly, both children fell asleep within a short time and the car was strangely quiet. Both of us were a little contemplative, still wondering what God was doing in our lives. We said little to each other as the miles passed. About an hour into the journey Paul felt a very similar sensation to the one he had experienced in his office about five days before. He was deeply conscious of the presence of God. Again, words began to flood through his mind and, just like the sentences he had so clearly heard earlier in the week, concepts became clear in his thoughts. So, clear, in fact, that within minutes he turned to Carol and told her that he knew exactly what it was that God wanted us to do. He told her that we were to train men and women and be part of sending them to the nations of the world. He explained some of the basic concepts and finally even said, confidently, that this new initiative would be called Africa School of Missions.

So clear was Paul's sense of leading that he sat down at the dining room table within minutes of arriving home and began writing as fast as he could. Within half an hour he had produced six pages recording all he felt God had told him. He recorded the name, stated some of the training strategies, spoke of mission and particular nations and described the initial processes in launching this new initiative. In retrospect, this was either an act of extreme presumption or it could only be ascribed to some clear and defining moment of God-encounter.

What was remarkable about those first pages in which the vision of ASM was described, is that they were written out of a vacuum. We had never run a training institution. We had no developed missiological thought and we certainly had no possible recourse to people or resources that could help make this vision a reality. In reality we were young, inexperienced people, not much past our mid-twenties with a huge amount of passion and very little else.

Following two remarkable, defining moments we struggled to identify what we should do next. As in every situation like this, the people we share our vision or impression of God's will with are vitally important. An uncaring or careless word at a time when a vision or leading of God is at its most vulnerable can have very negative affects. We were naturally cautious as the whole thing seemed so audacious, so presumptuous. South Africa was isolated both economically and politically at the time and the very notion of training and sending men and women into ministry in different nations around the world seemed ludicrous. We also did not want to destabilise the good work that was going on in the life of the local church.

We decided to seek the counsel of David Newington (mentioned earlier in chapter 6), whose help and advice had been vital at several key moments in our lives. We made arrangements to see him and could hardly wait for the moment to open our hearts to someone we knew we could trust. The morning of our meeting arrived and we began sharing our journey of the past few weeks. He listened intently and, when we thought that he would enthusiastically encourage us, he gave a response we had not expected. He simply stated that it was not for him to "mess with the chemistry of our souls whilst the Holy Spirit was at work." It seemed such a disappointing response, but time proved that it was wise and good counsel.

Thus began the quiet maturing of the vision that God had placed within our hearts. We cautiously shared it with a few close colleagues, but no one seemed particularly enthused. Some thought it was a good idea, but it was clearly a vision that could not work in South Africa. Others felt that the idea was a good one, but it was in the wrong place and certainly at the wrong time.

Amazingly, within the short period of just seven years everything that Paul had written on those six pages had come to pass and much, much more. Men and women who had trained at ASM were serving in over fifty nations around the world; new ministries to the poorest of people had been initiated; and a remarkable campus with dozens of great buildings had been established.

When God called us we had no idea how any of this would come to pass, nor any sense of the remarkable journey that we were about to embark upon. But we learnt valuable lessons about placing our trust wholeheartedly in God and having the confidence to believe that He will accomplish all that He purposes to do in and through us.

Endnotes

56. Exodus 3
57. Joshua chapters 5 & 6
58. Judges chapters 6 & 7
59. 1 Samuel 17
60. Isaiah 55:8-9

God Will Provide

Miracles of Provision

> "God's work, done in God's way, will never lack
> God's supply."
> —Hudson Taylor

> *"And my God will meet all of your needs according to His glorious
> riches in Christ Jesus."*
> (Philippians 4:19)

From about as early as we can remember we became aware of the importance of the story of God's faithfulness as spoken or recorded by others. Our home church encouraged personal testimonies and we heard the remarkable story of God's grace through the mouths of many ordinary people who had amazing stories to tell.

Somehow we also became fascinated with the biographies of great missionaries. People like C.T. Studd and Hudson Taylor were a huge inspiration to us. We remember the remarkable medical missionary story of Ida Scudder and later Paul Brand. The writings of Don Richardson influenced us greatly and the biographical history of the Church by Ruth Tucker helped give us perspective of the many and amazing lives of faith-filled people who had gone before us.

About the mid-eighteenth century Christian scholars, predominantly in the universities in Germany and Holland, tried to create natural divisions in the theological curriculum. They understood the need for what is normally referred to as *systematic theology*.[61] Another term used in this regard is *dogmatics*. In other words, these scholars saw the value in helping the wider Church define its doctrinal position. Defending orthodox doctrine is also known as *polemics*.

These same scholars also saw the need for biblical theology. Simply, this was the study of the Bible in such a way as to clearly identify the unifying themes that run through it. Their concern was to ensure that the Bible was not used as some other religious texts in a superstitious sort of way, by chanting one portion endlessly or misquoting another for the sake of some form of religious practice. They were concerned that good principles of biblical interpretation including issues such as context, background, linguistic forms and others were all properly used in identifying the way in which God makes Himself known to us.[62]

The third clear division in the theological curriculum at this time was known as *applied* or *practical theology*.[63] Issues such as how the Church should function, how people were effectively discipled and so on were included in this part of the theological spectrum.

The fourth category for describing Christian theology was Church history. Although there are different views about how we interpret Church history, and whilst their Church tradition or law affects various Christian groups differently, the understanding was that doctrine and practice develop over time and must therefore be placed into the context of history and evaluated as objectively as possible.

Without knowing the process of how Christian thought has developed throughout the centuries, we were deeply impacted by the narrative theology of many missionary authors. These books built faith inside our hearts and, more importantly, planted a deep sense of compassion inside us. We remember responding to every missionary challenge. Over just a few years we found ourselves passionately committed to God's world, willing to serve anywhere that He called us. We would watch ancient 16mm films (that normally broke down half way through the screening) and unashamedly weep as we were confronted with the needs of people who lived half a world away from us. We also chose to use as many of our school holidays as possible to visit an amazing mission station set high in the Maluti Mountains of Lesotho. Mt Tabor, as the mission station was called, played a huge formative role in our lives and the missionaries, David and Gretchen Kast, impacted us deeply.

Thus, by the time, we had experienced God's call to establish the Africa School of Missions there was already a deep deposit of missionary life and thought within us. It was undefined and incomplete, but we both knew by the time of Paul's experience with God in July 1983 that somehow a commitment to winning people to Christ everywhere would form a significant part of our lives. We knew we were called to the nations.

By late July we knew that God had awoken us to His purposes and that somehow this involved mobilising and training men and women. Our inclination was to find some form of property that could serve as our first little college campus. The thought was naïve and simple, but it certainly did not lack passion. We held hands and prayed together. We spoke into the small hours of the morning about all of our plans, from how we would feed prospective missionary students through to the innovative ideas we were developing regarding their training. It was exciting and daunting, especially considering we were young pastors in a relatively small church and there was no prospect of any significant resource being made available to us.

Instinctively, we responded to the many missionary stories we had read over the previous five years. We remembered the steps of faith, the courage and the determination of these ordinary people who had accomplished so much. As a result we determined that we would try to buy a piece of property and then recruit a small group of intrepid young people who would be prepared to give themselves to a couple of years of missionary preparation. Although we had little academic background ourselves we also knew that this program needed to be academically credible and deeply spiritual and practical, all at the same time.

We approached a real estate agent in the area that we were strangely drawn to ever since our first night away with our friends at the guest farm. It is still referred to as the Lowveld – an area about a four hour drive east of Johannesburg in South Africa's Mpumalanga province. It is a naturally beautiful area with hills and granite outcrops. It is subtropical with beautiful vegetation, dotted with vibrant and fragrant flowers that seem to grow bigger there than anywhere else.

Before long we were being driven to a number of small farms with large houses and we became more and more excited. In our enthusiasm every place seemed just right! We could envisage young people packing out each room in the old farmhouse, eager to learn and happy to sacrifice when it came to the standard of their living conditions. In fact, we became so enthused by the whole experience that we boldly made an offer on one of the farms, committed ourselves (and God) to much more than we could ever afford and then took the four hour journey home and waited in eager anticipation for the miracle to occur.

There was no miracle. In fact, within an hour of returning home we had a call to inform us that the farmer had rejected our offer and would not consider any further offer. We were devastated! This kind of thing did not happen in the books we read. It seemed from the books we had been reading that there was always some amazing form of provision that clearly and obviously demonstrated God was at work. Why was God not doing the same for us now?

Paul remembers retreating to his study with a heavy heart. Typically, all the questions about whether we had heard from God or not over recent weeks flooded his mind. Before long, disappointment took over and Paul quietly accepted that maybe he had not heard from God and that the excitement of the past few weeks had been purely manufactured because of his desperation to break out of the spiritual crisis he had endured for so long. He loved and honoured God enough not to get angry, but he did make it clear that he would no longer drive this vision forward and if it took three weeks, three months or even three years to come to fulfilment, that was fine with him.

It actually took just a little less than three weeks. Paul received a phone call and a nice gentleman introduced himself and said that he had heard that Paul had a vision for a missionary training centre. Immediately the vision sprang to life again and Paul shared his vision enthusiastically. This led to a dinner meeting at which more visionary thoughts were shared in an unashamedly passionate way. We remember well the evening that this gentleman we had just met, and about whom we knew virtually nothing, ate our dinner with relish, then got into his car, thanked us for our hospitality and drove off. We had no idea what was going on!

Sometime later we received another call and this time the same gentleman asked if it would be possible to arrange a meeting that would include his wife. Of course, we were intrigued by what was taking place and soon another meeting was arranged. Again we shared our vision with our new friends.

And so Gerry and Mary Schoonbee came into our lives. We soon met members of their family and began to discover the remarkable journey they had been on. Mary came from Scotland where she had been brought up as a devout Roman Catholic. Gerry was born in South Africa and had been raised in a strict Dutch Reformed tradition. They had met whilst Gerry was building roads in Zambia as a recently qualified civil engineer. Mary was a nurse serving there at the time. They soon fell in love and married on the understanding that their very different church backgrounds would preclude any conversations regarding religion or politics from their marriage.

Gerry was an astute businessman and over the years rose to the top of his field. He became the managing director of a large construction company. They raised their children sending them to Catholic schools and enjoyed the fruits of hard work and good financial management. As a result they had accumulated reasonable wealth.

In his early fifties Gerry was invited to attend a Campus Crusade For Christ breakfast, organised especially for business people. It was there that he was confronted with the clear and compelling understanding that Jesus Christ had died for him and that He wanted to lead Gerry's life completely. And so he became a fully devoted follower of Christ. His life changed so obviously that his wife soon enquired about the change and it was not long before she, too, was fully committed to Christ in a very personal way. They immediately began to commit their energy and resources to the great cause of Christ.

Some time later they became involved in some initiatives in the Lowveld and found themselves in a position to purchase a resort hotel built on about fifty acres of land. With continued financial investment and much effort they ran a conference centre for some time, but it was a huge financial drain. Thus, when they heard through a mutual friend of our vision they became interested to hear what God was leading us into.

In early October 1983 we met with Gerry and Mary in the

lounge of the conference centre known at the time as the Good News Centre. Again, we shared our vision, still not really aware of what the full potential of these discussions might be.

After copious cups of tea and long but happy conversations we will never forget that October day when Gerry leant forward and with quiet deliberation told us that God had given Mary and him confidence in our vision. They believed that we would be instrumental in impacting nations and that God would raise up hundreds of men and women and send them to needy people around the world. Finally, he stated clearly that in order to achieve these outcomes he and Mary would donate the entire property – from the teaspoons in the kitchen to the pool in the gardens, to Africa School of Missions. What a moment that was! The provision of this large facility with rooms, classrooms, large gardens and space for development was more than we could ever have imagined or dreamed. As if the donation of the property was not enough, Gerry and Mary committed resources and a year of hard work to refurbishing large parts of the complex, upgrading others and even the funds to build three houses. How could we ever thank them enough for their kindness and generosity?

Thus it was that we opened the doors to our first group of students in January 1985. Thirty-six intrepid men and women from several nations began their missionary training with us. We remember Peter and Eddie Russell-Boulton joining our staff along with their four children. Carol's brother Geoff committed to working with us and later her parents made a similar commitment. Over the coming years God sent us numbers of fine men and women who served alongside us in training people for ministry.

We began building the campus with houses and family accommodation. We added a large chapel and developed a library. We also began serving our local community (some stories are recorded later in this book). Over the years hundreds of people made their way to ASM for training and the work continues to thrive to this day.

Not everyone helped us, however, and some openly opposed us. But that is just how it is when you pioneer significant things. Life has gone by rapidly, our children who were so young when we began this college are now grown and our daughter has children of her own. They saw the very best in people and witnessed the worst in some. But we still stand amazed at the work of God in our lives at that time. We celebrate an involvement with missionary training that now spans three decades. We revel in our regular visits back to ASM and delight at the development that continues.

Along with the thousands of narratives of God's faithfulness to pioneers, apostles and humble servants of God who have committed to serve the cause of God's kingdom around the world, we humbly add our own story. It says exactly what they have all said: "Our God is a faithful God!"

Endnotes

61. A helpful book understanding these theological developments is J. K. Smith, *A Radical Orthodoxy: Mapping a Post-secular Theology* (Grand Rapids, MI: Baker Academic, 2004), pp31-61.
62. S. Grenz, *Theology for the Community of God* (Grand Rapids, MI: Eerdmans, 1994), pp2-6.
63. D. S. Browning, *A Fundamental Practical Theology: Descriptive and Strategic Proposals* (Minneapolis, MN: Fortress Press, 1996. He observes that practical theology has gone through a "rebirth" in the past 40 years. Osmer, *Practical Theology,* pp1-29 agrees that since the 1960's there has been a shift in practical theology. P. Ward, *Participation and Mediation: A Practical Theology for the Liquid Church* (London: SCM Press, 2008), p47 concurs with Browning and Osmer and says the discussion means that a "disembodied theology" now seeks to embody beliefs.

We Must Do Something!

*Overcoming the
complacency of inactivity*

"The purpose of life is a life of purpose."
—Robert Byrne

"Here is the test to find whether your mission on earth is
finished. If you're alive, it isn't."
—Richard Bach

*"Do not conform any longer to the pattern of this world, but be
transformed by the renewing of your mind. Then you will be able
to test and approve what God's will is – his good, pleasing and
perfect will.*
(Romans 12:2)

Finding the will of God has become almost an obsession with
some. We spend much of our lives with young people who are
starting the journey of Christian service and we cannot help
but notice the nervousness with which many of them try to
navigate the complicated theology they have developed around
exactly what it is that God wants them to do.

Since the Reformation about five hundred years ago, the
issue of discovering God's will has become an increasing challenge
for many Christians.[64] Add the importance of our individuality
– which has come to us through the thinking of those com-

mitted to the Enlightenment – and it becomes even more complicated. Before the Reformation people were told that all they needed to do was to unquestioningly obey the teachings of the Church, regularly take the Mass along with confession, and all would be fine. Understandably, the Reformers wanted to throw off this level of clergy control and began by establishing detailed theological systems called *systematic theology* or *dogma* to enable Christians to follow God and obey His will.

The one problem with this thinking was that the will of God seemed to many of the Reformers set and established. God decided things on our behalf before we were even born. Some of the Reformers seemed to suggest that everything was settled and predestined and that we had very little to do with choosing the pathway upon which we walked the story of our lives. As time went by this view was challenged, but to this day the Protestant Church has struggled to reconcile the will of God with the responsibility of man.

As Church history continued upon this trajectory different Christian groups began to believe that they were experiencing revival or, in some instances, a return to the New Testament pattern of church life. Examples in the English world would include the Methodist revival under the Wesleys during the 18th Century or the associated revival in North America often called the Great Awakening.[65] Towards the end of the 19th Century and spilling over into the early 20th Century there were the first reported accounts of what was to become the Pentecostal phenomenon, which resulted in thousands of churches being established around the world within one hundred years. However, with each new expression of God's grace in His Church, discovering His will seemed to remain elusive and complicated.

As young Christians we were taught to pray and fast in order to discover the will of God. This had the effect of reinforcing just how complicated it was to discover what He really wanted for our lives. We believe in prayer and fasting, but this is not the only way in which we discover God's will for our lives. Then there was the issue of prophecy or receiving a word from a respected Christian leader. We were eventually fully persuaded that there needed to be at least three significant signs such as a word, a particular Scripture (irrespective of its context!) and some form of confirmation – such as a prophetic utterance or some unusual financial provision – for us to prove the will of God. It was all quite exhausting, but we stuck with it because we did not want to offend God in any way.

The result was an almost crippling level of inactivity. We often did very little while we waited for yet another confirming action on God's behalf. This rather narrow and "mystical" approach to discovering the will of God was challenged one afternoon during the early days of our leadership of Africa School of Missions.

Paul walked into the living room of the house where we were living to find Carol on the floor, overcome with emotion. With obvious concern he sought to comfort her and all that he could hear between muffled sobs was, "We have to do something!" Something had deeply impacted Carol and Paul needed to know exactly what it was.

As she tried to regain her composure she began to tell of her visit to a local village, only about a mile from our home. We knew some people who lived there and had often provided transport to people who worked at the college to a junction with the main road just a few hundred yards from this particular village. However, on that particular day Carol found herself visiting in some of the homes and walking with a few of the women from the village. Within minutes she was made shockingly aware of the fact that there were large numbers of very young children taking care of their even younger siblings for hours each day, whilst their parents went in search of just enough work to provide basic shelter and clothing. Such a desperate world existed a stone's throw from our comfortable world and we knew so little about it. It was not uncommon to find seven or eight-year-old children caring for two-year-olds for eight to nine hours each day. Many of them were constantly hungry and their little faces and sad lives broke Carol's heart. Her shoulders convulsed as she tried to tell of the traumatic experiences of the day and Paul instinctively knew that our lives would be changed forever.

We learnt in dramatic fashion that the will of God is not some far-removed, mystical force that needs complicated spiritual processes to discover. However, this does need some further explanation.

Yes, we do believe that the specific will of God can be discovered through times of prayer and fasting – and oftentimes prophetic words can give necessary confirmation to that leading. We also believe that God's Word can lead and direct people in pursuing His specific will for their lives. God is a personal God and He longs for a relationship with His people, so He talks to us and we in turn talk to Him.

Yet, we can unquestioningly obey God's commandments, which are clearly taught in His Word, and still struggle to find His specific will for our lives. For example, we can believe in the principle of faithful and monogamous marriage, but still struggle in choosing the right life partner. So, there are times in a Christian person's life where they need specific guidance. But on this day we started the remarkable journey of realising that the will of God is also discovered in community, not only in the lonely recesses of our hearts. It is *doing* the prophetic thing that God has already shown us is good – to do justly, to love mercy and to walk humbly with our God.[66] We were learning that the New Testament pattern has little to do with the songs that we sing, the theology of our worship or even the kind of church that we attend or lead and it has everything to do with mission.[67] Outside of a total commitment to bring God's peace on earth we will always find the intricacies of discovering His will to be complicated and even elusive.

There are times when fasting for divine guidance is a necessary and important discipline in a person's life. There are also times when, out of zealous devotion, Christians will fast and pray for justice and peace. Then there are times where we find God's will just in our daily experiences of life. This should not appear contradictory. Rather, they reinforce each other in a commitment to living a certain life.

Put another way, without an extravagant commitment to love, care and give, the will of God becomes yet another expression of self-indulgence. The will of God for my life must be subject to the will of God for His world. It is not so important what God does for me, it is much more important what God does through me. Simply, we have to do something![68]

Inactivity will rob us of discovering the will of God for our lives. Withdrawing from meaningful Christian fellowship, an introverted spirituality and an existence on the fringe will completely destroy the full and certain life that is already God's will for us. Our advice is simple: engage with life and get connected. Just do something! Get to church next Sunday and engage with all that is happening with a determined effort. Live with obvious energy, commend someone for their efforts, undertake a spontaneous act of kindness and give with unbridled joy and generosity. This is the surest way to discover the perfect will of God for you. As the New Testament puts it: become a living sacrifice and so prove His perfect will.

That day in our living room changed our lives forever. Our theology became applied and not merely mystical. There is a mystical dimension to faith that is lacking in the Church and we do not want to discourage that element. We believe in a supernatural and mystical God who wants to accomplish the miraculous. Further on in this book you will read of how we as a family have encountered the supernatural and miraculous intervention of God in our lives on different occasions. We are not discounting that element of faith for a moment. We are stressing the importance of actively looking for more opportunities to serve and to live completely unselfishly. Carol arranged with a local pastor to use a simple church for a child-care facility. She persuaded some local farmers to give their overripe bananas to her and within days was caring for children. About twelve turned up the first day and by the end of the week there were one hundred and eighty. With just one local helper she cared for them, fed them and provided basic hygiene. They were exhausting days, but there was no alternative. Something had to be done. The love of God compelled her, leaving no second-guessing as to what the will of God might be. As the days turned into weeks Carol became aware of a subtle opposition to her work fuelled by the growing political instability in South Africa at the time. On her way home one day her life was seriously threatened and a group of angry young men tried to roll over the vehicle that she was driving in. Later their anger turned towards the church where her child-care centre was located. It was sadly burnt down and the work ground to a rapid halt.

Did she miss God's will? Of course not! Every day she fulfilled His plans and purposes. Each life impacted was worth the effort. Little children were given some respite and experienced just a moment of the dignity they deserved. As the work halted the seeds that had been planted fell to the ground and died. It took several years for them to germinate, but they eventually sprung to life again. As the political situation in South Africa stabilised so the opportunities for students and staff from Africa School of Missions developed again. By this time the HIV/AIDS pandemic had hit the eastern province of South Africa with devastating effect. Thousands were affected leaving orphans in many households.

We remember a Board of Directors meeting that was addressed by a doctor serving on the faculty at Africa School of Missions at the time. She told us of her morning that day. As she prepared her clinic she was asked to meet three children. They were all under the age of ten and all they had in their possession was an identity document for their mother. She had died very recently and these little ones had nowhere to go. After finding a volunteer to provide temporary housing she tried to get back to her medical work when a messy bundle was delivered to her door. Inside a sodden blanket was a little baby less than twenty-four hours old. Someone had gone to relieve themselves in the early hours of the morning, had heard a muffled cry and, on investigating, found this dear little baby in the sewage at the bottom of the long drop toilet. The doctor's plea to the Board meeting that day echoed Carol's words: "We have to do something!"

These experiences and others led to strategic efforts to provide home-based AIDS care, orphan care and a large clinic for critically ill people. Recently, a new facility for nurse training was opened at Africa School of Missions.[69] Did Carol find God's will? She really did. She discovered the best by simply being prepared to do something. This principle continues to help us govern our lives. We continue to take opportunities resulting in the capacity to do more than we might otherwise. But life is certain, full, overflowing.

Inactivity robs us of discovering the best that God has for us. Jesus leads us "in the way". His will is confirmed as we care for the poor and feed the widow and the orphan. Nothing compares with the passion that arises within the human heart as a result of primary obedience and committed activity. It is in doing something that the fuller will of God is revealed, adding layers of meaning to our lives and giving us the unparalleled liberty of loving and serving in an unselfish way.[70]

Endnotes

64. D. MacCulloch, *The Reformation: A History* (New York: Penguin Group, 2003). This book gives a thorough background to this period of history.

65. R. Hattersley, *John Wesley: A Brand from the Burning* (London: Little Brown, reprinted 2003). This book provides a detailed biography of Wesley's life and ministry.

66. Micah 6:8

67. Matthew 28:18-20

68. N. T. Wright, *The Challenge of Jesus* (London: SPCK, 2000), p131 says, "In the cross and resurrection of Jesus we find the answer: the God who made the world is revealed in terms of a self-giving love that no hermeneutic of suspicion can ever touch, in a Self that found itself by giving itself away, in a Story that was never manipulative, but always healing and recreating, and in a Reality that can truly be known, indeed to know which is to discover a new dimension of knowledge, the dimension of loving and being loved." He goes on to say that this is the vocation of all Christians, "... to tell the story, to live by the symbols, to act out the praxis ..." See also B. J. Walsh & S. C. Keesmaat, *Colossians Remixed: Subverting the Empire* (Downers Grove, IL: InterVarsity Press, 2004), pp129 see Colossians 2: 1-4.

69. www.ASM.org.za

70. Wright, *Surprised by Hope*, pp267-307.

Treasures Stored in Secret Places

Learning to live missionally

CHAPTER

11

"Expect great things from God; attempt great things for God."
—William Carey

*"And my God will meet all your needs according to his glorious
riches in Christ Jesus."*
(Philippians 4: 19)

An entire book of the New Testament was written by a missionary leader primarily to thank the kind donors in the church at Philippi for the way in which they had remembered him "again and again". This is a very personal letter filled with gratitude to a church that had generously supported the work of the first century apostle, Paul.

Christians are normally aware that the earthly ministry of Jesus concluded with a clear commission to His disciples to go into all the earth and lead others into Christ-followership.[71] The specifics on how it was to be done were never addressed by Jesus, but there can be no doubt that He saw His mission on earth being continued through the sacrificial work of His people.

In many ways, this was not a unique position held by Jesus. He was actually affirming the whole weight of what prophets and leaders had said from the earliest of times. A reading of the

Old Testament reveals a thorough missional theme. God assured Abraham that he would be the father of many nations.[72] Later, He declared that the temple should be a house of prayer for all nations.[73] A constant theme throughout the prophets is to take care of the widow, the orphan and the foreigner. God's relationship with Israel was never intended to be insular or exclusive. Rather, Israel was chosen to be a nation of God-reflectors.[74] Their uniqueness was not in their laws or their religious rituals, but in their sense of being reflectors of the eternal God who was before all things and would continue beyond the present age.

Many of what we normally refer to as the Prophetic books of the Bible were written specifically because of the failures of God's chosen people in being missional. Their greed and lack of compassion was offensive to God and He sent one prophet after another to warn of His anger. By this stage many Israelites could not imagine why God would be angry with them and so they stoned the prophets and did them great harm. One of the specific warnings from the prophets was that, if God's people did not care for the most vulnerable within their society then God would give them a taste of their own medicine. He would make them strangers in a foreign land. This happened and after a catastrophic invasion by the Babylonians where Israel was taken captive, thousands were led away into captivity. This period is known as the exile. It helps to understand which prophets were making their declarations before the exile and which were after the exile.[75] The main point, however, is that the greatest expression of God's relationship with us is not in how we use His favour to our own ends, but how we reflect this favour to a needy world. This is mission.[76]

So, when Jesus gave His great commission He was using familiar language to His first century listeners.[77] They were fully aware of Israel's call and now began to understand that this was the true messianic message – to take good news to all people everywhere. Within weeks the early followers of Christ had experienced Pentecost and almost immediately thousands from around the known world were responding to Peter's preaching.[78] It is not long before we hear of Peter having a strange encounter with God in which he sees a sheet lowered from heaven containing all sorts of animals and food.[79] As a devout Jew he would never eat such unclean stuff, but the message is clear: God declares that if He makes something clean it is clean. A day later Peter was in the house of a Roman soldier and the gateway to the Gentile world was opened for the Gospel.

In fact, most of the New Testament was written as a direct result of the expansion of the Christian message into a large part of the Mediterranean world. The ancient message of God's love was now embracing people of many cultures and languages. In order for this to happen, people began to travel and preach at every opportunity. There were many missionary journeys, some recorded in detail in the book of Acts and many never recorded at all. One of the more prominent of these travelling preachers was Paul. He was a pioneer. Drawing from the wealth of his Jewish background he entered this amazing new world of serving God in the power of the Holy Spirit. He was led to Macedonia and eventually had a passion to preach the good news all the way to Spain.

As we read of this first century expansion of the Christian faith two things emerge. The first is what we sometimes refer to as a Trinitarian understanding of mission. These early pioneers began to understand that as the Father had sent His Son, so the Son sent the Spirit and now the Father, Son and Holy Spirit send an empowered Church to reach all people everywhere.[80] This remains the driving force of contemporary mission.[81] Mission takes place when people are sent. The second thing to note is that, whilst God the three-in-one sends, God's people play a major role in providing for this enterprise.[82] This was Paul's experience with the Philippian church. Amongst their own projects and their concern for the poor in Jerusalem, they clearly saw the need to provide for Paul's ministry and living costs. A biblical precedent was thus set.

This model continues to this day. The Church exists for mission and as people follow God's leading into mission, so churches and individuals should willingly support them. We have been sustained in many different situations through the kindness of people and churches just like those in ancient Philippi.

And it has not always been just in the small things that we have proved the generosity of God's people. At times we have had to trust for more significant amounts as well. From time to time throughout this book we have referred to our time in leadership at Africa School of Missions.[83] We led this amazing college for ten years and have an ongoing involvement to this day. After just two or three years of training and raising missionaries on the beautiful campus, set at the base of the Legogote mountain, the facilities we had were clearly stretched to their capacity and we needed more buildings. Several new staff homes, new teaching and administration blocks, as well as upgrades to the kitchens and the workshops were all now urgently required in order to maintain the growth we were enjoying.

Of course, this required a large amount of money and, as a young leader, Paul was not sure how to go about raising these much needed funds. Typically he resorted to thinking of a thousand possible ways that it might be done. One option was to mortgage the property and simply pay off the loan over a long period of time. In our view, there is no biblical or theological reason why we should not incur some secured debt of this nature. Problems with our finances tend to arise mainly out of unsecured consumer debt or when the secured debt is clearly beyond the capacity of the individual or organisation to service it. Thus Paul practiced a speech that he delivered one morning to the senior leadership team at the college.

It went something along these lines: when someone needs to buy a shirt they go to a shirt shop. (All agreed that this was the case!) Likewise, if someone needs shoes they go to a shoe shop. (Again, all agreed – it was going well thus far). So, if someone needs money they go to a money shop – which is just another name for a bank. Paul's argument continued that the college needed money, so why did we not simply go to the money shop and buy some? At this point he was aware that he was losing the team he was addressing. The college had never incurred any debt and it was clear that no one shared Paul's enthusiasm for doing so now. The meeting came to an inconclusive end and Paul was left with the distinct impression that he was the only one who wanted to proceed down the pathway of buying some money and that this was not going to be the way forward.

As the team left Paul's office he could not help but have a sense of discouragement, almost despair. This was God's work! Why did it always seem such a struggle to take major steps forward? He resorted to a brief but honest outburst of complaint to God. In the midst of this rather pitiful time his door was suddenly flung open and with no ceremony or respect Carol rushed in. She began to tell of her encounter with God just minutes before. She had devotionally opened her Bible and, with little knowledge of what was transpiring in Paul's office at the other end of the campus, she had quietly asked God to open His Word to her. She opened her Bible to Isaiah 45 and began to read. We have never read the Bible as a series of disjointed promises to be "claimed" when they seem appropriate. There has always been a deep conviction that the Bible must be understood in its context. However, on this occasion there was clearly something remarkable happening. It was as if the Scriptures came to life and the verses began to speak powerfully to her. She felt as though God was applying these verses and they contained His promises for our situation.

When she reached verse 3, which speaks of God giving us treasures stored in secret places, she was convinced that God was giving us the reassurance that He had the funds required for all of our visionary expansion. Without hesitation she ran to the front door, across the college campus, through the building and into Paul's office. Between rapid breaths she told Paul what had happened and declared that there were treasures stored in secret places waiting to be discovered by us. All this occurred on the eve of a mission trip that Paul was taking to the eastern part of France. His first inclination was to believe that these treasures were spiritual and might refer to a positive response to his ministry in France. Carol was insistent: it was not souls, it was *money!* Over the next ten minutes Carol's passion and obvious encounter with God persuaded Paul – so much so that he arranged for a late afternoon staff meeting and, during that time, wrote the Isaiah scripture on a white board at the front of the room. Intriguingly, few in the room shared our enthusiasm and by the time we walked home at the end of the day we felt less than enthusiastic about the whole experience.

Paul packed his few belongings and left for France, a little uncertain about the events of the previous day. This was before emails and international phone calls and so Paul had very little idea of what his preaching itinerary involved. He had a letter saying that he would be met off the plane and looked after from that point on. True to their word, his hosts met him off the plane. Before they reached the car they informed him that a friend who now had his headquarters in Germany had arranged to have lunch with Paul that day. Paul commented on the fact that he had not even had a chance to shower, but before he knew it he was ushered off for a lunch appointment he never knew about.

The conversation was great. The two friends shared bits and pieces of good news and Paul suddenly found his typical enthusiasm for all that was happening at Africa School of Missions. Without warning his friend stopped eating, dabbed his mouth with his napkin and informed Paul that God had just instructed him to "sow a seed into Paul's ministry". Without any connection to the events of the previous day, Paul assumed that this would be a small contribution to the cost of his international air ticket. The meal ended quite abruptly and the two made their way back to the ministry offices where Paul's dining companion made a number of internal phone calls.

He then went on to explain that his ministry had a number of key projects planned for Europe, but God had clearly instructed him saying that if he took these funds and gave them to the college in South Africa that God would multiply them back for the projects they had planned. Paul was still not putting the whole picture together. A short while later he was handed a cheque that he graciously slipped it into his pocket. His friend quickly protested and insisted that he should see how much it was made out for. With emotion that was hard to check, Paul saw that it was for exactly the amount he had encouraged his leaders to take as a loan from the bank! It provided enough money to build five new staff homes, a beautiful new administration and teaching block, as well as new work-shops and other campus upgrades. What an amazing provision!

Carol had the joy of reporting the good news to the staff and there was great rejoicing all round. The leading of God had been proved by the provision of God. This principle remains a constant in our lives. If we are passionately missional – com-

mitted to God's cause in whatever way He may lead – we can
have the reassurance that God will provide for the journey.
Again and again we have proved God in this way.

There remain two important points to be made. The first is
to state again the incredible adventure that awaits those who
determine to live their lives in a missional type of way. This
simply means a reprioritising of our lives around the causes
that most touch the heart of God. A commitment to justice
and fairness, a compassion for the poor, a deep desire to understand the New Testament in its first century setting and a
willingness to be a positive participant in the life of a good
church all form a part of this missional lifestyle. A journey into
the theology of how a sending God, Father, Son and Holy
Spirit wants to direct His followers into situations where they
can bring redemptive change adds depth and dimension to a
missional commitment.[84]

The other point is that the need for the sacrificial support of
missionary activity is as great as ever. The biblical precedent
still stands. Local churches should allocate a generous percentage
of their funds to missional activity. Part of these funds should
unapologetically be given to release apostolic ministries around
the world. Warm relationships, such as the one between Paul
and the church at Philippi, enrich local churches. Those with
trans-local ministries need the answerability that such relationships provide. Thus, in the sending and the providing God's
work goes forward and His name is honoured throughout the
earth.

Endnotes

71. Matthew 28:18-20

72. Genesis 12.

73. Isaiah 56:7

74. Deuteronomy 7:6; 2 Samuel 7:23; Isaiah 42:6; 49:6; 60:6.

75. Jeremiah 5:19. The book of Daniel is central to the period known as the exile. Nehemiah and Ezra are examples of post-exilic books.

76. W. Brueggemann, *The Prophetic Imagination* (Minneapolis: Fortress Press, second edition, 2002) – a good read in relation to gaining insight into the prophets from a great Old Testament scholar. Wright, *The Challenge of Jesus,* pp18-34.

77. Matthew 28:18-20

78. Acts chapters 1-3

79. Acts 10

80. D. J. Bosch, *Transforming Mission: Paradigm Shifts in Theology of Mission* (American Society of Missiology 16; New York: Orbis, 1991), p390 postulates, "Mission [is] understood as being derived from the very nature of God. It [is] thus put in the context of the doctrine of the Trinity, not of ecclesiology or soteriology. The classical doctrine of the missio Dei as God the Father sending the Son, and God the Father and the Son sending the Spirit [is] expanded to include yet another 'movement': Father, Son, and Holy Spirit sending the church into the world." People like Karl Barth were advocating a Trinitarian base for the missional God long before Bosch wrote his seminal work.

81. Two helpful books in this regard are: A. Hirsch, *The Forgotten Ways* (Grand Rapids: Brazos Press, 2006). M. Frost and A. Hirsch, *ReJesus: A Wild Messiah for a Missional Church* (Peabody, Massachusetts: Hendrickson Publishers, 2009).

82. L. Newbigin, *Foolishness to the Greeks: The Gospel and Western Culture* (Grand Rapids: Eerdmans, 1986). On p9 Newbigin asks the question: "From whence comes the voice that can challenge this culture on its own terms, a voice that speaks its own language and yet confronts it with the authentic figure of the Crucified and living Christ so that it is stopped in its tracks and turned back from the way of death?"

83. The miraculous story of the birth and growth of Africa School of Missions is to be published in the near future.

84. M. Frost, *Exiles: Living Missionally in a Post Christian Culture* (Peabody, Massachusetts: Hendrickson Publishers, 2006). See also H. Peskett and V. Ramachandra, *the Message of Mission: The Glory of Christ in all Time and Space* (Leicester: InterVarsity Press, 2003).

Making Memories

Reminders and rituals

"It is surprising how much memory is built around things
unnoticed at the time."
—Barbara Kingsolver

*"Then Samuel took a stone ... He named it Ebenezer, saying,
'Thus far has the Lord helped us.'"*
(1 Samuel 7:12)

It helps at times to see the creative mind of the eternal God at
work behind the requirements that He makes of His people.
So often our religious inclination has made us concentrate on
the things that God's people can do and, more particularly,
what they cannot do. Thus, from time immemorial the following of God has, at times, been perceived as a rather legalistic
lifestyle filled with restrictions and limitations.

A deeper look into the ways of God shows a completely
different story. Although God clearly made specific requirements
of His people and continues to make requirements to this day,
the whole purpose is to enable us to live functional and fulfilled lives. If we view these "God-requirements" through the
lens of reminders and rituals it helps put them into perspective.

Much of the ancient law that we find in the first five books
of the Bible had to do with things that today we call civil law.

It had to do with degrees of relationship, much as contemporary marriage laws do. There was also basic hygiene, some aspects of which, if consistently applied, could well have prevented the devastating plagues that destroyed so many lives in Europe during the Middle Ages. Likewise, there were laws about sanitation, taxation, land and wealth distribution and multiple other very practical requirements that contemporary politicians still have to deal with.

Then there were the moral laws. The central expression of these is what we call the Ten Commandments.[85] They have to do with how we govern our hearts. They are pointed, uncomplicated and address the issues of our humanity in a very direct way. Keeping these laws enriches life and relationships, making life work. Ignoring or flaunting these laws erodes self worth and makes life dysfunctional.[86] Thus, a careful evaluation of the law that God gave His ancient people does not show Him to be some cosmic killjoy, determined to straightjacket His people and make them stand out like sore thumbs. Quite the opposite, God's law actually shows His care, His grace and His desire for His people to reflect the God they served.

Whilst the ceremonial law and most of the civic laws of God no longer apply to us because we are not a part of the political structures they were originally meant for, the moral law still applies. Of course, many of the ceremonial laws also had to do with ancient Israel's spirituality and their relationship with God through sacrifices and temple worship. These, thankfully, have all been fully satisfied through the atoning work of Christ on the cross. So, to help us understand the role of law and grace, contemporary laws have largely replaced the civic laws. Christ has fulfilled the ceremonial and religious laws and the moral law remains an obligation but, for the Christ-follower, it is not a rod for our backs. In fact, the amazing biblical truth is that the indwelling Spirit of God actually helps empower us to fulfil the moral law. For us then, we have the joy of living "loving the Lord our God with all our heart, mind and strength and our neighbour as ourselves".

Interestingly, one of the ways in which God tried to reinforce the creative and redemptive nature of keeping His law was by means of rituals and the making of memories.[87] A consistent theme throughout the Bible is the instruction God gives His people to celebrate seasons, keep certain rituals and do things to create memories. For example, there are specific rituals such as the keeping of the Passover.[88] To this day Jewish families remember this significant event through rituals that involve the youngest to the oldest members of the household. Then there was the instruction by God to remind the children of the household on a daily basis that there is only one God.[89] This is called the great "Shema" of Israel. In fact, the Jewish people take this so seriously that they have the practice of writing this verse on a small piece of parchment and then putting this inside a phylactery, or a little pouch, that is then bound daily to the forehead. The whole intention is to remember.

Jesus did exactly the same thing. His clearest instructions to His disciples related to partaking in the communion meal.[90] After sharing a meal He then took bread and broke it. As He passed around the broken pieces He told His disciples that this was symbolic of His broken body. He then took wine and required them to pass the cup from one to the other. As they did so He told them that this was a powerful symbol of His blood that was to be shed on the cross. Then He gave clear instruction that they should do this regularly in remembrance of Him. Clearly Jesus knew the importance of ritual and of making memories.

Reflective practice is lacking in many Christian circles. The Christian life is not only about "doing", it is also about "being".[91] Worship should include declaration: who God is and

how great He is – but it should also be reflective: stating how
kind God has been in our lives and how we should therefore
honour Him with our thoughts and our deeds. Even church
services should include elements of ritual, especially if we take
the biblical model seriously. These do not have to be complicated
or liturgical. It could be a routine moment of quiet reflection, a
regular prayer for a particular people group or the singing of a
benediction. The point is not the method that is used, but
whether we are passing a noble memory, a sense of communal
ritual on to our children and their children.[92] The memory of
God inside us is created both through Bible teaching and communal ritual. Instruction and reflection combine to produce
worship in the hearts of Christ-followers.

As we look back over our shoulders we realise that we came
to understand the importance of ritual and remembrance without
fully comprehending their true meaning. We embarked on
practices and family disciplines that fulfilled the need for ritual
and the creation of wholesome memories but, to be honest, we
did not do it by design. It was spontaneous but, as time went
on, we became increasingly grateful for these little family rituals
and practices. The result is some very happy memories, just a
few of which we share with you here.

For a long time we have held family "conferences". Paul has
always held the conviction that decision making should pass
through several stages. The first was a quiet, internal check to
make sure that the decision to be made was not based upon a
passing whim or a temporary fancy. Then there was the need to
pray and simply submit the matter to God, giving Him the
right to close or open doors as He saw appropriate. Then there
was the necessary conversation between us that would often go
on in various forms for days or even months. If the matter had
to do with our ministry choices we would normally involve
either the leadership team or a person who we respected.

Finally, once the process was fully developed, there was the final but very important requirement that the whole family was involved. Even when the children were very young we would ask their opinion and it helped us to explain the decision that was being taken in the simplest of terms. Of course, at a young age the children would sometimes respond in a shy way or express some special concern that was especially pertinent to them. They would almost always support us and we let them know that we really valued this support. As they grew older, the conversation became wider and more aspects were considered because of their participation. At times they expressed their reservations, but we discovered that over the years the discipline had established a high respect in their lives for our decision-making processes and for us personally. It would be true to say that they always knew this was not mere tokenism, but that their opinion was valued and, if their case was strong enough, could even change the whole process.

Another of these little rituals was our New Year's Day family conference. Each 1st of January Paul would buy delicious pastries from a local bakery. The coffee would go on, the best crockery would be brought out and we would settle down, often still in our pyjamas, to a morning of conversation, Bible reading and prayer. These were the most special of times. We would reflect on the year that had passed and then verbalise our hopes for the year that was ahead. At times we would admit to handling situations badly and ask forgiveness. We would always speak about mission and our call to reach the poor and the oppressed. We would often speak about budgets and the financial challenges of the coming year. We would always hold hands and pray. Whenever possible we still try to have these times, even though our children are now adults and Anna has a family of her own.

Partly as a result of these rituals and disciplines there were times when we agreed that we would travel together. This was always a very special time. Normally Paul would receive some form of invitation to preach at an event or over a period of time in a local church. Mostly these were events such as missionary conferences or leaders' and pastors' conferences. In an inexplicable way, from time to time, Paul would feel a conviction that the family should accompany him on one or other of these trips. By way of quick explanation, in the early days of our travel there were occasions when there was no specific offer of financial help. On some occasions he would purchase an air ticket and then trust God and the potential kindness of his hosts to cover the cost before he returned home. Sometimes this did not happen, but God would always provide in some way and we never found ourselves unable to meet all our financial obligations. On most occasions people were kind and through offerings and personal gifts he would always cover the costs of a trip. This was fine for one person travelling, but four people travelling was another story completely!

On one of these occasions Paul had been invited to a number of events including speaking at the opening of a school in a small town near Boston, USA. About a year before he had spoken at a midweek mission event in this church and they had been financially generous and helped to cover his ticket and expenses. The invite included several services over the weekend and so there was at least some confidence that this church would make a good contribution towards the costs of the trip, especially as they had initiated the invitation. Encouraged by this, a family conference was called and everyone decided that this was one of the trips where we should all travel together.

As the time for the trip grew nearer another piece of correspondence encouraged Paul. A good friend in Chicago had heard of our plans and offered to have us spend our last weekend in the States with him. He undertook to introduce us to another church or two and the hope was that these commitments would combine to help cover the costs of all four of us travelling.

Just prior to this happening we had been very encouraged by a massive financial gift we had received to help the work of Africa School of Missions (as recorded in the previous chapter). This further encouraged Paul, so he planned the three-week trip to include a visit to Disney World, which had always been a fatherly dream of his. The big day came and we left for Boston via New York.

We were welcomed by our friends and enjoyed their kind hospitality. The weekend was full with the school opening, the Sunday services, youth meetings and a lunch with the church leaders. As we made arrangements to leave the next day, an envelope was handed to Paul and the family could hardly wait to get around the corner to see how God had met our needs. To our dismay there was just a very small, token financial gift that was not enough to cover even the short commuter flight from New York to Boston. Paul did his best to conceal his deep concern, but within minutes had an overwhelming sense of peace. He then acted out of character. He told the family that we were going to have the best time imaginable at Disney World and that money was not an issue. To this day he cannot account for the source of his courage, except that somehow God was being an amazing Father to him in order that he might be a great father to his children.

The first amazing thing that happened was that the whole family was upgraded for the trip to Florida. Jason was convinced that this was God answering his prayers. We then had the most wonderful time and, for the first time before or since, Paul put the expenses on a credit card. We would never recommend this and it has never been a part of our financial management. But it was clearly part of a bigger plan that God was working on our behalf at that time.

Three wonderful, memory-making days passed quickly and soon we were on our way to Chicago. Our friend had arranged a nice place for us to stay and had made a car available to us. But he then broke the news that he had been unable to arrange any ministry engagements for us. He was awaiting a response from a small, pioneer church in Chicago, but apart from this there were no other opportunities for ministry. As we had felt dependent upon these services to help what appeared to be a dire financial situation, we were extremely disappointed. It was family conference time again and together we held hands, prayed and asked God for His help.

There was a little glimmer of hope when we received a call the following day to say that a service had been arranged for us at the little pioneer church. However, this was quickly tempered when we were informed that the attendance was seldom more than twenty people and that this could be far less because the following Sunday was Father's Day! We left early for the church as their meeting place was on Lake Shore Drive in downtown Chicago. There was little traffic, however, and we soon arrived and found parking with little difficulty. True to our worst fears, by the time the service began there was a handful of eight to ten people at the most. Paul remembers a surging feeling inside and turned to Carol declaring that this was going to be one of those days that we would trust God to make us a very special blessing to these people. Suddenly numbers seemed completely unimportant and we engaged the service with all our hearts.

As the service progressed we whispered to each other and agreed that we should encourage the little church with some of our stories relating to God's faithfulness. Carol stood up and began to relate how she had felt God speak to her out of the book of Isaiah chapter 45 and how this had ultimately led to a major financial breakthrough for Africa School of Missions.

She spoke of God's goodness and how He tests our faith but loves to show us His provision. As she sat down the Pastor made his way to the piano and we noticed that he was quite emotional, his eyes brimming with tears. Without saying anything he began to play and soon he was singing a magnificent song. We immediately recognised the words from Isaiah chapter 45. The pastor kept playing and then began to explain to the small gathering that he had been awake early in the morning. He had these words going through his mind, although he was not familiar with this passage. He later went to his piano and spontaneously began to sing the Scripture. As he sang in the early hours of the morning he felt God tell him that he would find out the meaning of the song during the course of the day. Carol's testimony had explained this plainly to him and he was completely overcome at the amazing way in which God had spoken to him. The key words in the verse related to a promise that God made to the king called Cyrus. He stated that He would give him *"treasures of darkness, riches stored in secret places."* We had already proved this to be true in our ministry and now this pastor knew that God was confirming a similar thing to him.

The service continued in this rather remarkable way. There was not a dry eye in the place. As we came towards the end of the service the pastor addressed the congregation. He said he believed that in order for the church to receive the "treasure and riches" they were seeking (which involved a new church facility), they first had to share their treasure with us, whom the pastor felt God had specifically sent to their church that day. One after another, individuals and couples began to contribute to a spontaneous offering being taken on our behalf. It was amazing and humbling all at the same time.

For some reason it took ages to count that offering. When they eventually presented our family with an envelope there was enough money in it to completely cover all the costs of our trip – every cent! It covered the air tickets for four people, our trip to Disney –everything. Talk about making a memory! Our children will never forget that moment and God's provision for us as a family. We had seen God meet the needs of our ministry time and again and now, once again, God was abundantly meeting our personal needs. We celebrated together with grateful hearts.

Again and again in difficult times our family has been able to remember God's faithfulness at that special time and remind ourselves that God can be trusted in any situation.

Endnotes

85. Exodus 20
86. Matthew 5
87. Exodus 20:8; 1 Chronicles 16:12
88. Deuteronomy 16:1
89. Deuteronomy 4:9; 11:19
90. 1 Corinthians 11:24
91. Stanley Hauerwas has written a helpful book in this regard. See S. Hauerwas, *A Community of Character: Toward a Constructive Social Ethic* (Notre Dame, IN: University of Notre Dame Press, 1981). Alistair MacIntyre highlighted virtue ethics and the importance of "being" over "doing". See A. MacIntyre, *After Virtue: A Study in Moral Theory* (Notre Dame, IN: University of Notre Dame Press, second edition, 1984).
92. In this regard Pete Ward's writings are useful. See P. Ward, *Participation and Mediation: A Practical Theology for the Liquid Church* (London: SCM Press, 2008) and P. Ward, *Selling Worship: How What We Sing Has Changed the Church* (London: SCM Press, 2005).

Whispers, Prompts and Nudges – part 1

Hearing God speak

"I am satisfied that when the Almighty wants me to do or not to do any particular thing, He finds a way of letting me know."
—Abraham Lincoln

"God does not work by only one method, paint in only one colour, play in only one key, nor does He make only one star to shine onto the earth."
—Eberhard Arnold

"Let's not be afraid to look at everything that has brought us to where we are now and trust that we will soon see in it the guiding hand of a loving God."
—Henri Nouwen

*"The Lord said, 'Go out and stand on the mountain' …
And after the fire came a gentle whisper."*
(1 Kings 19:11-13)

A significant part of the Bible is written in order for us to gain an insight into how God speaks to His people. In the earliest days there was a form of direct conversation with God. Clearly this occurred in the Garden of Eden, during which time our ancient forbear, Adam, enjoyed an unhindered relationship with God.[93] After the alienation of man from God due to a wilful and disobedient act, God did not stop communicating with people. He did so through signs and, at times, it seems as though people heard God's voice audibly. This was the case, for example, with Moses and his encounter with God at the burning bush.[94]

One trend is clear and that is that God spoke spasmodically to people and when He did it was usually in regard to a major event that He was orchestrating.[95] The Bible is not a fully exhaustive account of God's dealing with men, so it is likely that there are hundreds, maybe thousands of other occurrences when God spoke directly to someone. However, the Bible does provide us with a pattern and this suggests that God spoke to certain key individuals at certain times to bring about His plans through them.

Some of these individuals were made responsible to communicate God's word to others. Such were the prophets. These were men who had the ability to discern what God was saying and then express it to others. Mostly God spoke to people within the nation of Israel, but certainly not exclusively.

When Jesus began His ministry He had much to say about God's ways and His will. Significantly, He promised that one would come just like Him and this one – the Holy Spirit –would lead us into all truth.[96] In other words, the provision of God to continue speaking to people is clear. The pattern is that through various means, God's voice would still be heard and that the promise of being able to hear and discern His voice was now available to every believer.[97]

Trying to engage the supernatural is not an activity that is reserved for people of faith. In fact, there has always been a fascination for discovering the unknown. Millions around the world make their livelihood from divining the future, "communicating" with the dead and encountering the invisible world. This suggests that any interest in hearing in a spiritual dimension has wonderfully positive implications, but could also be open to abuse. God makes it clear in the Bible that His people should never resort to any form of witchcraft.[98] This is a kind of generic term that suggests that anything that uses real or imaginary communication from the invisible world to manipulate or control another is wrong and God detests the practice. This sobering truth makes the issue of how we hear from God a very important subject.

Perhaps a good way to continue the subject of how we hear God's voice would be to suggest a number of things that we should *not* do if we want to hear Him speak to us.

Firstly, we should never hurt ourselves in an attempt to have God speak to us. God conducts His relationship with people based upon His grace and love and never upon any sense of judgement or anger. We have strange remnants of ancient religious behaviour in contemporary Christian theology that suggest we should somehow do something to "please" God before He will be willing to speak to us. Throughout history people have beaten themselves, starved themselves or even lived under extreme conditions in an effort to have God speak clearly to them. Whilst their devotion and even their piety might not be questioned, their method should be questioned. The whole message of salvation through the full, atoning work of Christ reminds us that He has now made a way open to the Father and we should come confidently and boldly before God and make our requests known.[99] By extension, the way from God to us has been made open and we can have a strong and biblical faith that allows us to believe that God hears us and answers us.[100] He desires to speak to us and there is no requirement anywhere in the Bible that He will do so more clearly or more willingly as a result of us hurting ourselves in any way.[101]

Secondly, we must be very careful of superstition when it comes to hearing the voice of God. There is no provision in biblical writing for anything that smacks of a kind of séance. In other words, we do not have to alter our mood, create a special atmosphere, burn incense or sit in a circle and chant certain words in order to hear God. At times people of Christian faith have tended to use such mixed methods to hear God.

Missionaries understand the concept of "syncretism". This occurs when practices that were a part of some form of non-Christian religion are included in the worship of people who now confess to be Christian. I have met Christians who feel there is no harm in checking their horoscopes and wait for certain alignments of the stars before doing something they think is important. This is superstition and should never be practiced by people who have a vibrant, living faith in the eternal God through Jesus Christ. Saying the same word over and over again has little impact and only serves to psychologically impact us rather than open our hearts and minds to the voice of a loving God.

And then, we should take care to avoid stereotyping the way in which God will speak to us. For example, some people feel as though they must have a Scripture to confirm their sense of the voice of God. This is commendable, but should not be a precondition excluding any other form of God's voice being heard. Millions of Christians around the world believe passionately in the work of the Holy Spirit through what is termed spiritual gifts. These gifts include words of knowledge and wisdom.[102] In other words, people believe that God can confirm His voice in their lives through an insightful and supernatural utterance given by another. Again, this is commendable and to be encouraged, but discerning the voice of God should not become limited to such an utterance. We must celebrate the creativity of God and the fact that He can speak to us in many different and wonderful ways and that He does not always repeat His communication with us in exactly the same way every time.

So, we have established that there is a biblical pattern by which God speaks to us and that this pattern is a continuing one. We have also tried to be clear about what should not be a part of our searching after the voice of God. These principles have served us well over the years and we can now look back and see how, again and again, God has spoken to us. In fact, this book is full of such instances, but we wanted to add the truth that God speaks often through whispers, nudges and prompts. This is consistent with the biblical narrative and, if conditioned by the cautions we have already mentioned, leads Christians into a very exciting life knowing that we are not dependent upon good luck, a whim and a wish or even the "prophetic" insistence of other people, but that God can speak to us and show us His way and will.

An early leadership experience will help illustrate this. It involves several different ways by which God chose to speak to us very clearly. We were leading Africa School of Missions and, in our early enthusiasm, we willingly created opportunities of service for numbers of people. We were innocent and naïve and so sometimes trusted people who, if we had investigated more carefully, we would have discovered did not have a good track record when it came to Christian service. We have made this mistake a number of times in our leadership. We are glad that we still are able to trust people even though our trust has been misplaced before.

One particular individual was proving to be very trouble-some. The problem was, though we felt an "undercurrent" and had bad feelings about him, we were never entirely able to nail down one particular thing he was doing in order to confront the problem head on. We were aware of little meetings and the fact that some students and even some staff on the college campus were questioning aspects of our leadership, but there was nothing obviously divisive in the actions of this man. However, the general atmosphere left us in no doubt that something was going on and that, whatever it was, was causing division and dissension in a team that had enjoyed unity prior to this time.

We were obviously concerned and began to ask God for an answer. The following Sunday we were in our local church (generally a good place for God to speak to us) and someone in the congregation stood up, saying that they felt they had something to share that would be especially significant for someone present. They went on to quote a Scripture saying that God whispers his secrets in the ears of those He loves. We immediately felt that this was part of the answer. Later that week Paul was teaching a group of students. The class was not part of the normal academic program, but rather Paul was encouraging students to become proactive in affirming and helping others. He was explaining that many of the times that God uses people are spontaneous. In other words, some of the gifts of the Spirit can operate through us simply by us deciding to be responsive to God and praying with another or sharing an impression or passing on a word of encouragement. He then suggested that the students spend a short while quietly praying for one another. One of the young ladies who would have had no knowledge at all of the challenge we were facing approached Paul. She was obviously nervous, but felt that she had a Scripture to share. In her nervousness all she could do was whisper in Paul's ear and she went on to say that the Scripture suggested that soon, "he who troubles you will trouble you no more". It could not have been more accurate or direct. It gave us great courage. Within days, some specific issues emerged and Paul was able to openly confront the individual concerned. A month later he left the college and his influence came to an end.

This was not an isolated case. Again and again we have felt an inclination which has proven, in retrospect, to have been God quietly prompting us. Soon after our daughter Anna was born we received an invitation to speak in a number of churches in the United States. We were living in England at the time and had very little by way of financial resources. The cheapest way to travel was with one of the early budget airlines. This involved actually travelling to one of their offices, standing in a line that sometimes took hours to get through and then purchasing tickets that allowed access to the plane, but no more. There was no reserved seating, no food, not even drinks were included. Our little girl was only a few months old and the whole experience of getting to the USA proved to be quite traumatic for us all. The trip itself was exhausting with travel and multiple speaking commitments. By the end of the trip the thought of travelling back to New York from the Midwest, catching a taxi to the airline offices and then standing in line for hours just to get a cheap ticket was not at all attractive. To add to our concern we had been given many gifts for our new baby and so our mobility was restricted because of the amount of stuff we were carrying.

We prayed our normal prayers that morning and then added (in a half-hearted sort of a way to be honest), that we would be very grateful if God would help us with the rather traumatic journey that faced us. Our first stop was Chicago, from where we were due to fly to New York before having to purchase our tickets in the way already described. Carol left the plane carrying our baby and Paul followed carrying everything else! Once we had found a quiet spot for Carol to sit down and for Paul to offload the luggage, it was necessary to get our seat allocation for the onward journey to New York.

Paul made his way to the check-in counter. This was the easy part of the journey and he cannot remember any specific prayer that he might have uttered at the time. With only one person in front of him and a rather tight time schedule, he was looking forward to getting the boarding cards and making his way with Carol and Anna to the gate in order to board early. However, at that moment he specifically felt a spiritual nudge, a whisper from God. He felt God was asking him to get out of the line and walk to the end of the departures hall. It made no sense at all. But the feeling grew rapidly, so much so that Paul graciously offered his place to the person behind him in the line and walked to the end of the hall. There was nothing there and he felt confused and uncertain and, at a distance, Carol was clearly concerned that time was running out. Smiling bravely, Paul returned to the line, waved gently at Carol and waited again to get the boarding passes. When he was just one person away from the check-in counter exactly the same thing happened. After a brief internal wrestle with his own imagination and his sense of the voice of God he once again responded to the nudge he felt God was giving him. Again, there was no obvious reason as to why he should have to walk to the end of the departure hall. Feeling a little silly by this stage he returned to the line, waved at Carol and waited his turn. Time was passing quickly and a small panic arose in his heart that, if this check-in process did not go quickly, he and the family would miss the connecting flight.

Inevitably, the same thing happened for a third time. Again Paul responded and walked to the end of the hall. As he was returning, wondering how he was going to explain this strange behaviour to Carol, he saw a little sign which stated simply: "Jet save to London, still available". Intrigued, he approached the desk. There was no line and the helpful lady explained that their airline – a major carrier – had just a few seats left for the London flight. They were selling these at a bargain price. In fact, the price was less than the budget airline! Even better, the flight left directly from Chicago just two hours later. After a few frantic calls our luggage was retrieved from the flight we were already booked on, we received a full refund for the Chicago-New York leg of the journey and avoided the long and difficult process of standing in line in New York for our tickets. And, even better, we got a full meal service on board! It was with an amazing sense of relief that Paul made his way back to Carol who, by this time, was seriously questioning his sanity. We hugged, possibly even danced a little and then enjoyed one of the best flights we had ever had.

God does still speak to His followers. He might use whispers, nudges and prompts, but however He chooses to speak the outcome is always good for those who choose to hear Him. A certain life is lived with the knowledge that we do not make our way on life's journey with a bit of good luck and a hope for the best attitude. This kind of life believes in a God who is interventionist. He involves Himself in our daily lives and makes His will and way known to us. To our readers, we urge a heightened sensitivity to the voice of a loving God. We suggest a close consideration of your underlying theology about how God speaks and, if there are any remnants of superstition, to deal with them. God is made known to us as our Friend and Counsellor. His voice can still be heard today.

Endnotes

93. Genesis chapter 3
94. Exodus chapter 3
95. See Joshua 1:1-2, Judges chapter 6, 1 Samuel chapter 3 and Isaiah chapter 6
96. John 16:5-16
97. John 10:27
98. Leviticus 19:26, 2 Kings 17:17, 1 Samuel 28
99. Hebrews 9:11-15; Hebrews 10: 19-25
100. Mark 11:24; Philippians 4:6; James 5:15; 1 Peter 3:12
101. Hebrews 10:22; James 4:8; Philippians 4:6-7
102. 1 Corinthians 12

Whispers, Prompts and Nudges – part 2

The gift of discernment

"Discernment is not a matter of simply telling the difference between right and wrong; rather, it is telling the difference between right and almost right."
—Charles Spurgeon

"God never gives us discernment in order that we may criticise, but that we may intercede."
—Oswald Chambers

"And this is my prayer: that your love may abound more and more in knowledge and depth of insight, so that you may be able to discern what is best and may be pure and blameless until the day of Christ."
(Philippians 1:9-10)

In the previous chapter we showed that there is a biblical pattern describing the ways in which God speaks to His people. We also showed that there is no reason to believe that this pattern does not continue and that we can still hear God speak to us. Another layer in discovering the voice of God for our lives is through an understanding of what the Bible calls "discernment".[103]

Put simply, discernment is a "God-whisper" that allows us to have uncanny insight into situations and people. It is a remarkable inner-compass that allows Christ-followers to have a deep assurance that they are not just imagining things or hoping for the best, but that they can have God's insight relative to the situations facing them.

There are several ways in which this gift of discernment can operate and it is worth describing them briefly. Firstly, there is what might be termed the charismatic gift of discernment.[104] This is a special empowerment by the indwelling Holy Spirit in the lives of His followers. It can actually be quite dramatic in that insights and understandings can be given to someone about another person or a pending circumstance that could never be known in the natural realm.[105] At certain times this gift of the Spirit can even assist us in discerning the unseen or spirit world.[106] There are numerous evil spirits that operate in this unseen world. Some can be very ugly and evil and have been known to hurt and harm people and families.[107] The circumstances around some people's lives are so destructive that they cannot be ascribed to bad choices alone. Those who operate with the gift of discernment will often be able to have a perception of what is really happening and can then, through prayer and committed fellowship, see individuals and even communities come to wholeness and greater functionality.

This gift operates in our lives at other levels. Especially for those in Christian leadership, but not exclusively, this gift enables us to have some insight into the motives of others. Not everyone who volunteers for some form of Christian service is motivated by the high and honourable ideals of serving Christ and doing people good. Some go from church to church or ministry to ministry and appear gifted and able until, after being trusted with a responsibility, they are found to be divisive. These people wreak havoc in churches around the world. It is difficult to say just what exactly motivates them, but it is not hard to see why the ability to discern or uncover their motives is a great asset to any Christian leader. The actual discernment might operate differently for different people, but the outcome should be to protect God's work and His people from damaging and divisive individuals.[108] It could be just an inner whisper that should not be ignored. It might be the absence of any sense of peace and this, too, should never be ignored. At times this gift even operates at a more corporate level – for instance when a team of leaders find it difficult to reach consensus and, rather than perceiving this to be the obstructionist behaviour of one or two, it could be that some have a heightened sense of discernment and thus the larger group should take heed.

There is also a more general way in which this ability or gift operates and that is at a day-to-day level where there is just a far greater sensitivity or awareness to things that are not evident to the physical eye. It is a whisper or a nudge, a quiet inner sense which allows Christ-followers the reassurance that God is with them and that He is leading them. This is not some mystical state that causes us to walk around whispering Bible verses constantly. Neither does it engender some form of suspicion about everyone and everything. This gift operates at its best when it creates freedom. God never gives gifts that somehow reduce us to suspicious individuals who can never trust others. Everything God does is to equip us to live better, serve better and help to create redemptive communities in which Christ's love is made known.[109]

Over the years we have seen this gift at work in our lives on many occasions. We have been very grateful for the times when this ability has aided us in our responsibility as Christian leaders. As young leaders we were not always able to understand the need for discernment. Often our enthusiasm would cause us to trust people beyond what was reasonable. Of course, this often created distress for us and the ministry we were leading. In retrospect, we remember the little prompts, the discomfort, the concern about private meetings that were taking place, but our naivety and lack of experience prevented us from taking courageous and decisive action. That is why it is important for younger leaders to value the counsel and friendship of those more experienced in life and Christian service.

In one rather dramatic instance we saw this gift at work. After months of divisive and difficult behaviour by a certain gentleman who had come to work with us, Paul became persuaded that it was time to ask him to leave. It was difficult because this man's actions were not outwardly wrong, but it was clear that he was badly influencing others who were working with us and there was a constant, draining undercurrent in our ministry environment. One young lady, who we had helped and supported, came angrily to Carol one day to state how much she hated Paul. It was unnatural, unprovoked and very unkind. This, along with months of similar serious and worrisome situations, led Paul, with as much grace as possible, to ask the man and his family to curtail their activities and to leave the ministry within thirty days.

Unknown to us, the man rapidly called various directors who had overall responsibility for the ministry we were serving in and within a week Paul was called to a rather adversarial meeting in which he was accused of being high-handed, immature and completely out of place in asking this man to go. It was difficult for him to defend his position except to try to explain (apparently vainly), the many instances of division and discomfort that we had felt within our community. At a point where it seemed as though nothing could be said to defend Paul's actions, one of the elderly members of the Board of Directors quietly spoke up. He had some previous experience with the man concerned and had, some years before, asked him to leave his (the director's) ministry. He simply stated that he had discerned a "familiar spirit" was at work. He went on to explain that this man had a long history of causing division, had a doubtful Christian experience and that unnatural and even sinister things often occurred when he became involved with Christian ministries. Immediately, the rest of the directors fell silent, looked at the elderly man with keen interest and the whole tone of the meeting changed dramatically. Two things had happened. Firstly, the older member of the Board had correctly discerned the dynamic of the meeting and had appropriately explained what was really behind the contention. Secondly, he had, over a period of time, discerned that this man, whether well-intentioned or otherwise, had a level of spiritual activity going on in his life that caused chaos whenever he was involved with Christian ministries. The New Testament often refers to the work of evil spirits. It seems as though some are wicked, others more benign. The lesson Paul learnt that day is that sometimes these unseen forces can work even within the context of a Christian ministry. The gift of discernment will assist leaders in minimising damage or preventing the influence of such forces in the first place.

Carol has consistently shown the advantages of having a sensitive heart to the promptings of God. Throughout our lives she has discerned situations and, as time goes on, she has inevitably been right in what she sensed. Some years ago we relocated to the United States to begin a missionary ministry. It was a big move for us and we arrived in a new country relatively unknown, trying to initiate a whole new work primarily into Europe. We certainly felt vulnerable, especially as we only had visas that would expire within three years. It was possible to apply for permanent residence status but Paul did not like the idea of yet another load of forms and the possibility of legal fees at a time when we were living with minimal financial resources.

Within weeks of taking up residence in a little home that was offered to us for a one-year period, Carol felt a sense of urgency about our long term position in the US. She shared it with Paul who, though he should have known better, countered her by saying that it really was not an appropriate time. He was considering the financial restraints we were in, but Carol was insistent. It was more than a motherly emotion or a passing concern – it was an inner whisper, a sense that God was at work.

Eventually Paul came to agree with Carol and, somewhat reluctantly, contacted an immigration lawyer. The lady was most helpful and asked about our family. Our son Jason was twenty years old at the time and there was only about four months before he turned twenty-one. At that point he would not be eligible for permanent residence as a result of our application and it was unlikely he would be able to stay in the US over the long term. The prospect of a family separation due to this regulation was not pleasing at all. We were already facing a similar situation with our daughter Anna. The lawyer asked for our papers and immediately began working on our permanent residence – often referred to as gaining a Green Card. We began to hear horror stories of friends who had waited in limbo, unable to travel for years. Some were stating that the process could easily take three to five years and by then it would be too late. Even the sense of urgency that Carol had regarding the application now seemed to have come too late. There were anxious moments, urgent phone calls and we prayed consistently for God to give us favour. As the weeks dragged on it became increasingly likely that we would not meet the deadline, which was Jason's twenty-first birthday. Carol consistently reminded the family that it was not just a passing urge that she had felt. She had distinctly felt the nudge of God and she intuitively knew that God would not tease us.

As often happens during stressful times, whatever can go wrong inevitably does! We were only one day away from the deadline and we discovered that all of our files had gone missing. We were sitting in a dingy government office waiting for an interview when we received this news. We waited for a long time with sinking hearts. Our attorney was a clever lady and she immediately made representation on our behalf stating some obscure law that, under certain circumstances, duplicate copies of documents could be used. She had wisely brought her files and her argument eventually prevailed. We were ushered unceremoniously into a small office, interviewed by a government worker who clearly was not enjoying her job, and about half and hour later left with the paperwork showing that we had been granted our Green Cards – all with less than eight hours until midnight and the final cut off time for Jason! We proved again that He who starts a good work will bring it to completion.

Some years later, Paul received notification through the post that he had held his medical insurance for two years and this now entitled him to a "well-man" check up. His first inclination was to throw the notification away. He hated going to the doctor when he was ill, so why would he ever want to visit the doctor whilst in perfect health? Somehow he mentioned this to Carol. Again she felt the strong internal compulsion that Paul should not ignore this and that he needed to make arrangements for the check up as soon as possible. The typical pattern ensued with Paul doing his best to dissuade Carol and avoid the check up, whilst acknowledging her sense that this was more than just a good thing to do, it was in fact what God wanted him to do. Carol's voice prevailed and Paul sheepishly made his way to the doctor's office. Exactly as he had predicted he was in perfect health. And then, also as he had predicted, the doctor requested some further tests including a stress test at the local hospital.

Recognising Carol's "God-whisper", Paul made his way to the hospital and undertook a battery of tests. All went perfectly well. He was, as he had thought, in complete health. Towards the end of the tests the doctor in attendance required a scan, which again appeared to show that everything was perfect. As it was all coming to a close Paul overheard a slight tone of anxiety in the doctor's voice. The doctor went on to inform Paul that he felt certain that the scan had shown a small abnormality in his aortic valve called a bicuspid valve. This, he went on to explain, meant that Paul's main valve for blood exiting the heart had just two flaps instead of the normal three. It was not something to be over-concerned with, but it might mean slightly less efficiency and should be monitored from time to time.

Some months later we relocated to the UK and, almost in passing, Paul mentioned this to his local doctor. Again, there was no alarm but the doctor suggested that it would be a good idea for Paul to see a specialist. The pattern became a familiar one – nothing for alarm, a slight abnormality, most people live and die with this condition and not from this condition. However, each visit prompted another test or another scan. After months a final scan was ordered which involved a camera being put down Paul's throat. It was a most uncomfortable experience and as Paul sat up and wiped his eyes following the scan, the doctor who had performed the procedure enquired if he had any pain in his chest or his back. Paul had no pain whatsoever. He was shocked to hear the doctor say that if there was any pain at all he would not allow Paul to go home as he had a very dilated aortic aneurism. This is a potentially fatal condition and Paul was reminded not to pick up any heavy objects and see another specialist as soon as possible. The appointment was set and this new specialist confirmed the findings and in a rather forthright way told Paul that his life was in danger until some rather dramatic surgery was performed to repair the extended aorta. Then another problem was discovered. An MRI revealed that the aneurism had extended beyond the junction with the carotid artery (the one that takes blood to your brain) creating a serious challenge for the surgical team.

Months went by with a constant anxiety within our hearts. Further scans were required and eventually Paul was admitted to the Northern General Hospital in Sheffield, England. Soon after being shown to his bed the anaesthetist paid Paul and Carol a visit. He went on to explain that this complicated surgery was scheduled to take fifteen hours. This was the first we had heard of this length of time! He explained that they needed to cut into Paul's shoulder to gain an alternative blood supply to his brain. They would then pass his blood through a heat exchange to cool it down and when he reached fifteen degrees Celsius, they would simply shut down all the life support machines and perform the surgery whilst Paul was clinically dead. He said that they had about a twelve-minute window to replace the root and valve of the aorta, suture up all the arteries that connect to it and then revive Paul and slowly warm him up again.

With that Paul was sedated and remembered very little until he awoke in intensive care where he needed to remain for four days because of the severity of the surgery. It was an anxious time for Carol and the children as they waited for news from the hospital. Thankfully, the whole procedure was a complete success and after two to three months Paul returned to work with as much energy as before.

Again and again we marvel at the sense of discernment, the nudge, the whisper that God gave Carol. We have come to trust His voice more than ever. Whether in leadership, relationships or life, the discerning work of the Spirit of God is one of the most comforting elements of His work within us.

A certain life is not without uncertainty or even trauma. The difference between a certain life and one lived simply by good luck or chance is that deep assurance that God knows and He is able to forewarn, grant peace or remove peace and speak in multiple ways to help us through whatever life throws at us. People who live certain lives develop a growing sensitivity to the nudges and prompts of the Spirit. They grow in their confidence in discerning situations and even people with the help of the Holy Spirit.

Our lives have been characterised by a consistent whisper from heaven. We have learnt to trust God's voice more. Our theology has become more certain. We understand God's will and ways more than ever and live with a deep gratitude that our God is not some distant eternal force, but is a Father who loves, who cares and who still speaks.

Endnotes

103. Proverbs 2:1-5, 14:16, 17:25, 17:28
104. 1 Corinthians 12
105. Acts 5, 8:26-40, 9:10-19
106. 1 Corinthians 12:10
107. Mark 5:1-20
108. Acts 8:9-25. Ephesians 4:11-12. In this regard Neil Cole is helpful in motivating us regarding the importance of being part of an organic community. See N. Cole, *The Organic Church: Growing Faith Where Life Happens* (San Francisco, CA: Jossey-Bass, 2005).
109. Romans 12: 1-2

Permission is Ours to Give

CHAPTER 15

The remarkable freedom of protecting ourselves from the effects of hurt

"To love at all is to be vulnerable. Love anything and your heart will certainly be wrung and possibly broken. If you want to make sure of keeping it intact, you must give your heart to no one, not even to an animal. Wrap it carefully round with hobbies and little luxuries; avoid all entanglements; lock it up safe in the casket or coffin of your selfishness. But in that casket – safe, dark, motionless, airless – it will change. It will not be broken; it will become unbreakable, impenetrable, irredeemable."
—C.S. Lewis

"Let us fix our eyes on Jesus, the author and perfecter of our faith, who for the joy set before him endured the cross ... "
(Hebrews 12:2)

Over the years we have discovered large numbers of people, many of them leaders, who have been restricted in their ability to lead certain lives because of the accumulation of internal hurt and disappointment. Books on the subject abound, but still it seems that many find it difficult to get over offence. The result is an overcautious approach to decision-making and a cynical view of the motives of others. This can be slightly debilitating to some, but crippling to others. However it affects us, the result is undesirable. We learnt that when it comes to the hurt of offence, the ones who hold the key to preventing the debilitating effects of it are ourselves, and that it is up to us whether we give the permission to others to offend us or not.

Throughout our lives we have often found ourselves initiating something with a significant visionary edge or reengineering a ministry that has developed unnecessary baggage along the way. Both of these responsibilities tend to draw more than their fair share of critics. As the temperance of maturity has settled within our souls we have come to realise that these critics are not necessarily bad people and they certainly do not deserve to be condemned or have our angry prayers said against them. They are often people who find change difficult or live with nostalgia.

Those who join a visionary movement are often hoping for some form of gain from the momentum that vision creates. Whenever such people later disagreed with us and verbalised their opposition, we used to take it personally. We would have long discussions between ourselves checking our motives and searching our hearts. We wondered why it was so difficult for these people to see our good intentions and our desire for long term good. This heart-searching only seemed to add to our confusion and hurt. Words can harm us. Sometimes they cut deeply and, after time, they build up internal inhibitions that make the next courageous step of leadership all the more difficult to take.

We remember well our efforts to reengineer a local church. We carefully analysed the problems, sought wise counsel from peers and then established a careful process for transformation. We contended that some structures were no longer serving the church well and had to go. This inevitably involved a changing role for some individuals. It also involved a fairly significant process of trying to keep as many as possible well informed.

Typically there were some misunderstandings. Sadly, some were expressed in rather angry, almost bitter ways. People who should have known better were saying unkind and at times, untrue things, and rumours of dissident groups meeting to discuss their concerns began to come to our ears. It all seemed like such an over-reaction to something that was intended to help us all and enhance the witness of the church to the community. It also proved to be more painful than we had anticipated. There were sleepless nights.

Paul came home one afternoon after facing a number of these subtle – and sometimes not-so-subtle – expressions of opposition. What made things so much worse was the sense that these unkind statements seemed to question not only our strategy, but also our motives. It hurt us deeply. It was at this low point that we learnt one of our key maxims for life and for leading.

We still are not sure what prompted Carol to say what she did. Standing behind the breakfast bar in our lovely home she simply said, "We don't have to give them permission to hurt us!" That single sentence was life-changing. What had she just said? Simply, her insight was that the permission for people's ability to impact our lives is ours to grant. A part of our self-awareness is to hold the key to our hearts and keep our dignity in all situations. We often refer to this as freewill. However, because this term has been caught up in centuries of theological argument, we tend to view it almost exclusively in regard to our responsibility in choosing Christ as Saviour. It is so much more than this! The incredible creative purpose upon our lives is to know God's acceptance and forgiveness and to live this knowledge out in all we do.[110] This does not result in some form of superficial arrogance or self-assurance, but rather a deep, inner confidence that we are born for a purpose, and that we occupy our place in time and space because of the loving,

providential plans of an immensely caring God. The result? We
choose the degree to which people enter our lives and influence
us. We are not some form of living technology that can be pro-
grammed at the will of others – we are purposefully created
and the grace of God is more than enough to equip us to be in
control of our hearts and our dignity. So, simply, in that
moment, we held hands across the breakfast bar and quietly
affirmed what God had shown us. We refused anyone the right
to gain access to the inner part of our lives and control us
through hurtful actions or words. And, amazingly, from that
day to this no one ever has! This does not mean that we do not
sometimes experience feelings of disappointment or discouragement. At times we even know what it is like to be distressed.
But, since that day we have learnt to carefully assess any potentially hurtful words or actions. We learn lessons that need to be
learnt, but refuse to let them penetrate our hearts in damaging
ways.[111]

This does not mean that we are now immune to pain. We
are human and as Lewis says our hearts are vulnerable. And if
we do "lock [them] up safe in the casket or coffin of selfishness"
then our hearts will become "impenetrable, irredeemable". We
do not want to put up walls and barriers and shut people out
of our lives. What we do is to ensure that even though we
cannot protect ourselves entirely from hurt, we can manage it,
so that it does not cripple us and cause irreparable damage to
our hearts. We cannot control situations, people or the words
they speak. But what we can control is the response of our
hearts. We can choose not to allow bitterness and unforgiveness
to settle upon our souls.

There are no guarantees for the future. God promises provision
for today,[112] guidance for today[113] and He promises that He will
journey with us in each day.[114] He never promised that there
would not be difficulties, hardships and challenges.[115] We

cannot control our futures. There were many people who thought they were financially secure, but when companies like Fannie May, Freddie Mac and the CEO's of large banks got greedy they soon discovered that their life savings were threatened and they had no control. Some people have a lie buried deep in their psyche that insists that if they follow certain principles then certain outcomes will be ensured. So then, if they look after themselves they will never get sick. Or if they work hard, everything will be fine. If they invest in relationships then there will never be a problem. They believe that if they just trust Jesus they will always be healthy and wealthy. This is simply not true – and neither is it biblical. The truth is we cannot control our lives. What we can do is relinquish control to a loving God who will walk with us through the challenges, difficulties and also the joy of our Christian lives. We can also choose our attitudes in the midst of each and every situation – because ultimately we control the responses of our hearts.[116]

The result of this decision has been incredibly liberating. Breaking the power of offence has been one of the greatest insights to living a certain life that we have ever had. To be honest, we still get mad at people from time to time. In fact, we sometimes get exasperated but, wonderfully, we never give permission to allow offence to cripple us and destroy the spiritual life inside of us.

In the Old Testament God gave very clear instructions on how His dwelling place, called the Tabernacle, was to be built. It had several clearly demarcated zones, each with a specific purpose and each having particular instructions regarding who could gain access to them. There was the outer court, which was accessible to almost everyone. Then there was the inner court, which could only be accessed by those offering sacrifices[117] – in other words, the act of repentance allowed more access. Then there was the actual covered zone that had two compartments. One was called the inner sanctuary or Holy Place and it was there that the priests fulfilled their constant duties. The other was called the Holy of Holies and only the High Priest was granted access to it. The details of this architecture contain numerous types or shadows of God's dealings with people throughout the centuries. It became the basic model on which the architecture of the Jewish Temple was based and, to some extent, has influenced religious architecture to this day. More importantly, it describes a model for the Temple of God, which is our own hearts.

Put simply, if we take seriously the statement that we are the temples of the Holy Spirit, then we too have certain zones into which we should allow differing levels of access to different people. The outer court of our lives should be filled with people – peers, acquaintances and even complete strangers. A certain life is not lived in isolation, but engages people, is interested in others and loves the diversity of the human race. It is in this space that we engage as wide a circle as possible. Those who live certain lives *love people*.

However, we should be astute enough to know that we can only sustain a certain number of friends in meaningful relationships. These then enter the inner court. They are allowed there because of mutual expressions of trust and friendship. These are the ones that form the circle that we call "friends". The relationship is mutual with shared respect. A friend does not always take, he or she gives as well. Some of these friendships are made deeper and more lasting by sharing at the altar of sacrifice – such as when people see us through a particularly difficult period. People who live certain lives are realistic about friendship and try not to presume upon others. The inner court is relatively well populated and so the expectations of the relationships that we enjoy with those that share this space must be limited.

Then there is the Holy Place. This place is reserved for very close friends and family. Again, those who live a certain life learn to value these relationships and work hard at them. They share the ceremonies of life together – praying for each other, keeping the lamp well trimmed, and eating together.

Finally, there is the Holy of Holies that is restricted and extremely special. We learnt that only the two of us and God belong in this space. It is this space that we guard most carefully. It is in this place that we celebrate the marriage we have, the love that we share and the faith that we cherish.

We have learnt that each of these zones has keys. We have also learnt that the ones who hold these keys and use them are *us*. It is our creative purpose to determine who enters, who gains access. The insight gained that day across our breakfast bar was that the permission granted to people as to how and where they have access to our lives is entirely ours to give. We can *know* many but be *friends* with fewer. Some are prepared to share the journey of life in a way that others are not and so, through trust and time, they enter the deeper recesses of our lives. We have also learnt that some have no right to enter the inner sanctuary of our lives where God has His throne and we share our love.[118]

Effective living and good leading requires that we mature beyond knee-jerk, reactive decision making into that confident yet humble posture of life that carries no hurts, is not easily offended and reflects God's grace. A realistic understanding of relationships characterises those who have made the correct and astute decisions required to live a certain life. We engage the wide world of people without allowing offence to cripple us and wound our spirits. There is no racism here, no blatant nationalism that separates the world community into those who are for us, or those that are against us. We love people equally, we care for those who suffer injustice and we refuse to protect our own comfort at the expense of others[119].

We are equally realistic about friendships, knowing that we only have the capacity to sustain a certain number of special relationships. We refuse to be hurt by those who choose to exit the inner court of our lives because of time or people demands.

By contrast, we cherish the Holy Place where close friends and family play a special part. We hold the key to this place, allowing a capacity to handle the disappointment that sometimes even those closest to us cause. We develop high levels of tolerance because these are the people we love the most. We let them into this special place and we love and serve them as a result. Finally, we guard the Holy of Holies. We guard the sanctity of our own hearts if we are single and of each other's hearts if we are married.

It is our choice who enters which zone of our lives and we take the responsibility to manage that zone with honesty and integrity. The result is a certain life lived without the debilitating inhibitions caused by hurt and unforgiveness. "Permission is ours to give" remains a significant maxim by which we live and enjoy certain lives.

Endnotes

110. M. Volf, *Free of Charge: Giving and Forgiving in a Culture Stripped of Grace* (Grand Rapids: Zondervan, 2005). In this book Volf weaves his theology of grace and forgiveness around his own personal story and the story of the Balkan people. Tom Wright, *Simply Christian* (London: SPCK, 2006), pp12-14 gives examples of great Christians who have paid a price for justice and freedom.

111. M. Volf, *The End of Memory: Remembering Rightly in a Violent World* (Grand Rapids: Eerdmans, 2006). This autobiographical narrative is a fresh approach to loving those who do us harm or hurt us. It places memory in its rightful position and helps us to resolve conflicts. Anderson, *The Shape of Practical Theology*, pp291-310. "To err is human to forgive is Divine." p291.

112. He promised the Israelites enough for today Exodus 16. When they did not trust Him and gathered more manna than He commanded it rotted.

113. Numbers 9:15 says that God would guide them with a pillar of cloud by day and fire by night.

114. Joshua 1:5; Hebrews 13:5

115. Romans 7:3-11. St Paul understood this well – living for Christ did not mean that there were no hardships.

116. M. Scott Peck, *The Road Less Travelled: A New Psychology of Love, Traditional Values and Spiritual Growth* ((New York: Simon and Schuster, 1978), said, "Life is difficult. This is a great truth, one of the greatest truths. It is a great truth because once we truly see this truth, we transcend it." p16.

117. Exodus chapter 40

118. Wright, *Simply Christian,* chapter three.

119. Volf, *Exclusion and Embrace*, pp22-31.

Stuff Happens

Growing through tough times

"Trials teach us what we are; they dig up the soil, and let us see what we are made of, they just turn up some of the ill weeds on the surface."
—Charles H. Spurgeon

"All the days ordained for me were written in your book before one of them came to be."
(Psalm 139:16)

Though our journey has had its fair share of challenges, nothing could have prepared us for what we were to face in the summer of 2002. We had recently relocated to Charlotte, North Carolina, in order to establish a base for our missionary commitment to Europe. Kind friends had opened a door of opportunity for us to have some office space for our ministry and we had even been able to buy our own little home.

Both of our children were attending university at the time and had returned to North Carolina for the summer. Jason had managed to buy a car and was planning on starting the new semester in a university in Southern California. In order to save for the long trip to the west coast he had been working wherever opportunities arose.

On the 1st of July he, along with Carol and our daughter, Anna, sat down to a typical summer lunch of cheese and tomato sandwiches made from crisp, fresh bread.

Understandably, he ate with relish and after devouring the first sandwich asked for a second helping. It was then that he remembered he had a small cheque which needed depositing in his bank account. He rose from the table, made his normal complimentary remarks about his mother's food and headed for the door. For some reason that we have never been able to understand, he raised his hand and with a broad grin looked at his mother and sister and said, "Love you more than life itself!" and disappeared through the door.

Some weeks before Anna had begun to go through a number of unusual experiences. It began with a deep, inner sense that God was preparing her for a special season. Over the weeks this sense continued and by the time she returned home for the summer she could remember several occasions where she had sensed God's work in her. As she returned home she actually began to feel ill and neither she nor Carol could work out what was making her feel that way. Then she had two very disconcerting experiences within the space of a few days of each other. The first took place when she looked out of her bedroom window to see her brother driving away. She felt compelled to run down the stairs and ask him not to go, thinking that possibly something could happen to him. She quickly pulled herself together and wondered why she could be having such a silly thought. A few days later she was sitting in the family room watching TV and thought she saw a terrible accident on the screen involving Jason's car. She jumped to her feet to ask where Jason was and at about the same time he actually walked into the room. Again she was confused. What had she seen? Why was she feeling this way? Later she wrote a little prayer in her journal: "Jesus, please protect my brother."

Jason took his normal route to the bank. As he crossed a notoriously bad intersection about a mile from our home his car collided with a fully loaded garbage truck on its way to the landfill site. We were told that the truck weighed over sixty-thousand pounds and was travelling at about sixty miles per hour. The full force of the truck rammed into the side of Jason's car. The impact was so great that it sheared the wheels from their axles. The momentum of the truck pushed the car sideways for more than the length of a football field and as the car and truck mounted the sidewalk, the truck flipped over crushing large parts of the car. In fact, the whole front and side of the car were flattened to the height of a shoebox on its side. The console had exploded into Jason's ribs and we were later to learn of the terrible injuries that he suffered as a result.

For some unknown reason, a first response medical crew were parked in their vehicle precisely at the accident site. They had no real explanation for this when we spoke to them later. The accident took place right in front of them with the car and truck passing within two feet of their vehicle. Before the dust had settled there was someone at Jason's side. They were immediately aware that they had a critically injured patient and called for a helicopter to get him to hospital. He was listed as a "G3" on the Glasgow scale, which is very critical indeed. He was not breathing, there was no pulse, nor any other sign of life.

Carol had gone about her normal chores and had returned home from the grocery store. It was a beautiful day and she had made some coffee and was preparing to enjoy the afternoon. The doorbell rang and Carol was confronted by a police officer. She could not imagine why he was there, but he quickly got round to enquiring if she was Jason Alexander's mother. He asked about his car and then broke the awful news that Jason had been involved in a horrendous accident and that we should rush to the hospital. Thus began one of our longest and darkest nights ever. In that moment of absolute darkness and despair Carol was reminded of Psalm 139:16: *"All the days ordained for me were written in your book before one of them came to be."* She knew in that moment that God knew about this day and somehow through the tragedy He would be with our family.

When we arrived at the hospital they would not tell us whether Jason was dead or alive. They confirmed that the helicopter had brought a patient in but, due to the litigious nature of American society when it comes to the medical profession, they would divulge nothing else. We paced the hospital feeling surges of desperation rise within us. Carol sat in a corner, placed her head in her hands and quietly whispered through her heartache and tears, "God, I am not prepared for this." Where was our precious boy? Would we ever see him again?

It took all of half an hour before two ashen-faced doctors made their way down one of those long corridors and asked to see us. The first words out of their mouths were to let us know in no uncertain terms that people with the injuries that Jason had sustained do not survive. Paul felt the blood drain from his face and had to rush out and splash cold water over his head. Carol felt every imaginable fear rise within her. It was at about this time that Anna joined us, having been driven to the hospital by her employer. We held each other's hands and quietly prayed and openly wept.

It was suggested that we go to the fifth floor of the hospital whilst the doctors decided how to keep Jason alive just a little longer. As we left the little room where we had received such devastating news something most unusual happened. Anna felt all of the illness that she had experienced for almost a week go and with a quiet internal resolution she turned to her Mum. They both stopped in the corridor. Anna placed her hands on Carol's shoulders and in a broken but certain voice said,

"Mummy, my brother is going to walk out of this hospital." The moment passed quickly, but the impact of those faith-filled words was immense. Little did we know at that moment that there was still more bad news awaiting us.

We were shown a small but private little room on the fifth floor of the Carolinas Medical Center. People were kind and compassionate, but there was an uncertainty and an internal pain that nothing could quench. By this time news had spread around the community and within an hour we were amazed to emerge from the room and find nearly forty people gathered to support us. We were a part of the First Assembly of God in Concord, North Carolina, at the time and their care and concern will never be forgotten. Members of the ministry team were there; others had bought refreshments for us. People who had been working with Jason in a retail store had left work and were standing alongside us. It was quite overwhelming receiving that level of love and support from a community that we had been a part of for only a few brief months. Our pastor, Sam Farina, and his wife, Vicki, stood by our side throughout and we had this deep, unspoken gratitude for the support of good Christ-followers.

Two more doctors asked to see us. They were both cardiologists and although they were obviously as professional as they could be in telling us of Jason's newly discovered injuries, their faces told us that they had little hope of saving his life. We discovered that the impact of the accident had been so great that Jason's heart had literally been thrown about inside him resulting in the rupturing of his aorta. The aorta is the major blood vessel leaving the heart carrying newly oxygenated blood to the rest of the body. A small membrane had somehow kept small amounts of blood flowing, but this injury was more than enough to kill him. Then they had discovered that one of his ribs had smashed inwards penetrating the atrium of his heart, plunging through both ventricles. It was as if Jason had been stabbed with a large dagger. The doctors asked us to quickly sign consent forms as they had to immediately undertake critical and hopefully, life-saving surgery.

We remember our pastor offering to pray for them as they left. They seemed to welcome this and, from the corner of our eyes, we saw them pray together a little distance down the corridor. The next few hours dragged by. People were kind and we felt wonderfully supported, but the internal agony was indescribable. It was at about this time that the earliest thoughts about the ways of God began to enter our minds. What we were experiencing was not something we had ever thought would happen to us. These things always happened to other people. Should God have prepared us better? Do bad things happen to good people? These and a thousand other theological thoughts would have to be deeply processed over the coming weeks.

It was 11.00pm before we actually got to see Jason – almost twelve hours after the accident. We were ushered into the trauma intensive care unit. Although it was late at night and there was little activity, we were aware of being with many very sick people. Life-support machines were making their unmistakable hissing sounds, there were beeps from respirators and monitors and about a dozen desperately sick people lined the ward. Jason was at the far end and we could hear our own footsteps as we anxiously approached his bed. How could we ever describe the emotion of that moment? He was lying there with tubes through his nose, breathing apparatus down his throat, intravenous lines in his neck and arms and by this time he had so many liquids inside him that he was bloated almost beyond recognition.

A kind male nurse was patiently administering syringe after syringe of platelets and plasma into one of the intravenous lines. We later learned that he had lost so much blood that a vital blood supply to his spinal column was interrupted. The doctors suspected that if he survived, he would be paralysed as a result. In fact, Jason received forty-two units of blood plus copious amounts of platelets and frozen plasma in the first thirteen or fourteen hours after the accident. That is equivalent to six or seven complete blood transfusions!

The nurse encouraged us to speak to him. Paul went behind the bed and lowered his mouth to Jason's ear. With emotion making it difficult to say much, he assured Jason of our love and of God's grace and whispered loving words into his ear. Carol looked for just one small part of his body that was not hurt or used for pipes and found a small spot on his forearm. She gently stroked it as tears flowed freely down her face. We did what came naturally to us. There was nothing manufactured or superficial. We loved our son dearly, we believed in a gracious God who knows best and so we responded as spontaneously as we knew how. We lived each minute rather than trying to fathom the whys or the wherefores of the situation. We later learnt how deeply this had impacted the medical team that so professionally stood by our side treating our son.

And so twelve short hours had changed our lives forever. The next chapter will record the rest of this amazing story and one day it might even occupy a book of its own. Never had our faith been plunged into a deeper challenge than these twelve hours had produced. Emotions, deep agony and faith all crashed together in our hearts, almost as violently as that truck had crashed into Jason's car. We felt our humanity and it was very painful. Within hours Paul's forearms had come out in a sore rash as the nerve endings there became raw. Each day brought another turn and another deep challenge. However, we learnt much about God and His people during that time.

We learnt that stuff happens, but that never changes the

eternal character of God. Our perspective changed from one in which we had somehow considered ourselves as temporal beings waiting for eternity, into one in which we gained the insight that we are actually eternal beings passing through time. Weeping endures for a night, but for those whose hope is in the eternal God, joy does come in the morning. And this joy is not dependent upon a specific or desired outcome. We faced the prospect on a daily basis that we could live the rest of our lives without Jason. However, we were comforted again and again by the fact that the "Lord gives and the Lord takes away" but His name is still blessed.

In other words, there is a constancy that sustains Christ-followers that is far more stable than the situations we are living through. We genuinely discovered this. The Bible refers to this whole dimension of the faith-life as having a peace that passes understanding. The person who has found an authentic faith in the resurrected Christ does discover an inexplicable level of internal tranquillity that has no basis in reason. It is not gregarious, loud or false. It does not make high-sounding statements or embarrass those who don't share that faith. It is a quiet, internalised confidence that, though much happens for which there is no explanation, the great and eternal plan of God will one day be made known. We discovered this amazing aspect of God's grace again and again.

We were grateful for the many times we had attended church, sat through sermons and sang the many songs that were included in our worship. Line upon line of truth had entered our lives. It was just a little here and a little there, but the overall impact was that some degree of spiritual maturity had developed and this is what sustained us through this painfully difficult time.

We also discovered that God's people are at their best in times like this. The church that we had served for just a short period rallied behind us. There were food parcels waiting at our home each day for nearly two months. Some amazing people set up a prayer vigil in the hospital that continued day after day. How can you say thank you for this level of kindness and commitment? The only way is to be willing to do the same if the need arises. Some of our deepest friendships were forged over the hospital canteen tables as people sat with us hour after hour and day after day. We discovered that conferences in different parts of the world were interrupted to pray for Jason and us. Thousands of emails poured in making us realise that every little investment we had made in ministry over the years was now being repaid.

Stuff happens. We live in an imperfect world. But every now and again we are given the privilege of seeing a little ray of God's amazing love and the kindness of His people shine through. We discover that life is uncertain, but that it can nevertheless be lived with confidence. This Christ-following life is not an artificial hope in the hereafter, it is a reality in the present. We are so glad for the peace of God, we are so grateful for the Christian community. We learned to value both over the few hours this chapter has described and over the months that lay ahead.

Her Hands in His Shoes

Faith and family in the toughest of times

"A woman asked a silversmith about the verse in Malachi 3:3: 'How do you know when silver is fully refined?' He smiled and answered, 'Oh, that's easy. When I can see my image in it.'"
—Unknown author

"He will sit as a refiner and purifier of silver."
(Malachi 3:3)

After leaving Jason's bedside at about midnight we were offered the use of an office on the ground floor of the hospital. It was cool and we quickly realised that we needed some provisions to get us through the night and hopefully the coming days. While we were waiting for updates, good or bad, it was agreed that Paul and Anna would drive home and pack a small bag with a few extra items of clothing.

It seemed like a long journey back to the house. We deliberately went on a route that would not take us anywhere near the accident site. Both Paul and Anna felt numb, so neither said much. It was not nice being away from Carol and the very recent memory of seeing Jason bloated and fighting for his life was deeply etched in our minds.

Paul packed a few items in a bag and rushed out of the bedroom to find Anna and get back to the hospital. The next few seconds brought another wave of emotion and made a lasting memory of one of those rare parenting moments. Initially, Paul could not find Anna but did not have the internal strength to raise his voice. He looked quickly into her room but could not see her there. And then a slight movement caught his eye and he looked into the darkened room across the passage. This was Jason's room. He could make out Anna who was crouched on the floor and in the next instant overheard her whisper: "Lord, please let my brother walk in these shoes again." It was then that Paul noticed that Anna had her hands inside a pair of Jason's shoes. Biting his lower lip and doing his best to control his emotion he quietly reached out for Anna's hand, lifted her to her feet and the two made their way back to Carol who was waiting anxiously at the hospital.

There was no sleep that night. At about five in the morning Paul went up to the intensive care unit, but was not permitted inside. Everything was tense and uncertain. There was very little news and it was not until nine that we were finally allowed to see Jason. Little had changed in his condition, but as Anna and Carol stood by his bed Paul was taken into a little room and again required to sign paperwork. It was then that the huge catalogue of Jason's injuries began to become clear. Apart from his heart injury he had a badly ruptured liver and an equally damaged spleen. Most ribs had multiple fractures, he had a broken arm and a nose injury. His lungs were also badly punctured and still bleeding. Everything possible was being done to just keep him alive.

Things seemed to go from bad to worse over the coming forty-eight hours. Infection set in and there was a great concern about pneumonia. In fact, it was eventually decided some days later to do a tracheotomy to assist life support. On the first

Wednesday we were surprised by a visit from most of the ministry team from our church. We did not realise, but they had been alerted to the fact that the medical team did not think that Jason would make it through the day and they came to support us. We gathered in the hospital chapel and wept and prayed together as we waited anxiously for the next little bit of news. It was a moving but agonising time.

The first week passed in a blur with everyone amazed that Jason was still alive. Then we received some devastating news. Jason had suffered three strokes during the course of one night. Fearing a set back the medical staff had taken him in for a scan and the result was not at all good. We were not going to go home that night until we had spoken to the specialist. He was undertaking emergency surgery and so it was not until eleven o'clock that night that we got to see him. Two remarkable things occurred within the next half an hour.

The first was in our conversation with the kind doctor. He gave us the information that he had about Jason's condition and confirmed that some clots of blood had broken away from either an injury or surgery site and had gone straight up the carotid artery and passed through his brain. It was at this time that they began to realise that Jason's heart injury was greater than they had thought and that there was still a large hole between his two ventricles, meaning that some blood was passing directly through his heart without going through the pulmonary artery to the lungs. This was possibly the reason why he had suffered these strokes. The doctor then went on to make a remarkable statement. He told us that he was not a man of faith and did not believe in God or the supernatural – he was a man of science – but he was, however, one of the surgeons who had been present on the day Jason was first air-lifted to the hospital. He looked at Carol and told her clearly that he had no understanding as to how Jason was still alive and that whoever we were praying to was doing more for him than all of those in the hospital. He then kindly suggested that we commit Jason to the care of our God and go home and rest. The ungodly was giving the godly good counsel!

The second unusual thing occurred immediately after this event. As Carol was regaining her composure and wiping her eyes, Paul went back into the intensive care unit. He stood at the base of Jason's bed near to the nurse's station. As he fought back the emotion, watching his son struggling for life, the nurse behind the desk got his attention and asked if she could say something. She went on to say a somewhat emotional thank you. Paul was taken aback. It was much more the case that we should thank them and not the other way around. He asked why she felt she wanted to thank us. What she said was amazing. She said that the team had watched us carefully. They had noted the way in which we were always there, always concerned, always touching Jason's arms and always whispering in his ears. She admitted that they did not see this often and it had touched them all deeply. She then fought back a tear and said that they were commenting on how the atmosphere had changed and that the medical team seemed to be getting on better! Then, amazingly, she told Paul that their records seemed to indicate that people were recovering quicker! She had no explanation. She did not want to attempt one – she just wanted to say thank you.

Although these experiences were thrilling, they did not dampen the pain or the uncertainty. In some ways they added to the emotion, but they certainly were a constant reminder that something was happening that was bigger than we could conceive at the time. The support of family and friends made a huge difference. Carol's brother flew in from India and her sister made her way from Australia as quickly as she could. Other friends travelled in to be with us too. Each made a lasting contribution to our lives and showed kindness, helped with meals and other menial tasks and poured love into our aching hearts.

The days dragged on. First one week and then another went by. We agonised with families as some lost their loved ones and rejoiced with others as their sons or daughters were transferred to less critical care because they were obviously getting better. It was not long before Jason was the one who had been in the trauma intensive care for longer than anyone else. We found ourselves invited to pray for many and did so with the empathy that nothing less than our own experience could have created. The hospital became a second home, the medical team our extended family and we were learning lessons of faith and appreciating each other more each day.

On the twenty-first day it so happened that there was a lovely Christian nurse caring for Jason through the small hours of the morning. She noticed a little movement and realised that Jason was quietly emerging from his coma. She told us in detail what happened over the next few minutes. She got up quickly from her position at the base of his bed, went to his side and began talking to him. She asked if he could hear her and was certain that he was responding. Taking his hand she asked him to move a finger if he understood what she was asking. He moved his finger! She then told us that the rest of the medical team began to gather around his bed. She asked him to put out his tongue, which he managed to do. She then told him that the next request was the most important of all. She asked him to wiggle his right toe. The whole team watched anxiously and to their amazement and delight he managed to do it. She then asked him to wiggle his left toe and again he was able to do it. He was awake, he could understand and he was not paralysed as they had feared. She told us the next day that there was not a dry eye around his bed at that early hour of the morning.

As we entered the unit the next day his resident doctor raised his hands high above his head and there followed a hugely emotional hour in which Jason recognised us and we were able to speak to each other for the first time in three weeks. He could only move his lips as the tracheotomy prevented him from actually speaking, but we understood each other. He was visibly relieved when we told him that the truck driver had not been seriously hurt and that there was no blame being laid for the accident. He told us he loved us; we told him we loved him. We stood with arms around each other as we celebrated the return of a son and a brother. Anna had been like a tower of strength to us throughout. Somehow though, in the tension and trauma of the past three weeks, we had all forgotten her prayer as she knelt over his shoes on the terrible night of the accident.

About a week passed and Jason was transferred to another part of the hospital and then about a day later we were visited by the doctors from the rehabilitation hospital. This was another amazing moment. They looked at the huge files they had brought with them and then looked at Jason. They conferred with each other and then told us that they could not understand what they were observing. Although Jason was frail and very weak, they could not believe that the boy in the bed before them was the same person described in the files. How could he have survived? They also suggested that he would be ready for rehabilitation within a day, but warned us that we should be prepared for a long journey, probably four to six months.

We walked alongside Jason's bed as he was moved to the rehabilitation hospital one building away from where he had been for the past month. By this time we had seen the huge wounds across both sides of his back where the life-saving surgery had been performed. We were conscious of his gaunt form and the tiny, spindly legs that were all that were left of his once strong, athletic ones. A month of induced coma had atrophied his muscles and he was now going to need to rebuild his strength slowly and painfully. A few days later he was sitting up and just a few days after that he was standing for the first time – bent, bowed and trembling, but standing nevertheless!

Then began the process of taking his first painful steps. His sense of humour returned. He remembered one of his grandfather's weak jokes and asked the doctor if he would be able to play the piano when the plaster cast came off his arm. The doctor replied that of course he would, to which Jason responded, "That's good, because I couldn't play it before the accident!" We were never sure if the doctor appreciated the humour.

After preparing ourselves for months of rehabilitation we were amazed when we were told just twelve days later that the medical team had assessed Jason and believed there was not a lot more that could be done for him and that we should take him home. Of course we were thrilled and woke up that morning with an overwhelming sense of joy, gratitude and excitement. We packed up a little bag for Jason with some clothes and a pair of shoes. We arrived at the hospital, dressed him and went through the formalities of signing him out. It was a moment we will never forget.

The hospital orderlies were called and a wheelchair requested. We waited and waited, but the chair never came. Eventually Paul stood up, challenged Jason and suggested that we walk to the car. Paul took one side, Carol the other, and Anna carried all the bags. Slowly but deliberately we walked the length of the corridor, rode down one floor in the lift and made painstaking progress towards the front door where our car was waiting. As Paul lifted Jason's legs into the car after having put him on the front seat he was suddenly overcome with emotion. The shoes he was wearing were exactly the same ones his sister had prayed over about seven weeks earlier! Then we remembered, "Mummy, my brother will walk out of this hospital." What a moment! It had all come to pass.

Theologians refer to study of the end times as *eschatology*. There have always been different views on exactly how things will work out in the final days and when Jesus will come again. Christians tend to agree on the fact that there will be an end of this earth as we know it and that the second coming of Christ will be closely related to this event. However, what happens beyond this has been confusing and even divisive. What is often overlooked in the debate is that no part of the New Testament Scripture is written in such a way as to create fear or foreboding relative to the end of the age. In fact, we are urged to encourage one another with the thought and prospect of Christ's second coming.[120]

Eschatology should not be based on a popular song, a series of novels or the ranting of a prophetic type of preacher. It should rather be a quiet, internal expectation that God the Father is in complete control and that He alone is the one who will decide when this world, as we know it, will come to an end.[121] It is this reflective yet powerful conviction that makes eschatology realised.[122] In other words, the future and present merge into a living hope, a sure confidence – a certain life. There is no need to live with paranoia about God, waiting for one moment of weakness before He allows the last trumpet to be sounded and we all appear before Him in fear and trembling. Rather, we condition our lives and live well every day with this eschatological hope pounding inside of us. This is another way in which His life is made real inside our lives.[123]

Perhaps this is one of the lasting and rich legacies that we have taken into our lives following Jason's accident. Each day is rich and special. Each family moment is a unique opportunity.

Each special occasion is another celebration. We have learnt to live unselfishly doing all that we can to make God's kingdom come on earth as it is in heaven. This is what the prospect of Christ's second coming should do. It should create hope; it should ensure that we live each day with purpose. Some of the petty issues that affected our lives before Jason's accident hardly ever enter our thinking now.

We have become more committed than ever to seeing the values of God's kingdom expressed on earth. The demands of justice and mercy consistently flood our hearts.[124] We passionately spend much of our lives mobilising people to the great mission of God, bringing hope where there is hopelessness and healing where there is pain. We travel often, take our students with us on mission trips and constantly challenge the innate selfishness that has crept into Western expressions of Christian faith. We have an eschatology that gives us hope for the future but passion for the present. The hope of eternity is the message of our lives. We refuse to live only for some uncertain, possibly far-off day, when we will be taken out of this messy world. It is this messy world that Christ died for and has given us the privilege of living in. Men, women, boys and girls all deserve to experience that same internal hope that we have.

We have learnt that values are much more important than vision. Loving the sick and caring for the aged are kingdom values that we hold dear. Caring for and helping orphans and widows are amongst the values most dear to our hearts. We still love being visionary and believing for a better future, but we also realise that all the goals and dreams we could ever have are meaningless outside of a well-developed value system and deeply imbibed morals. It is these values that we constantly instil into our students. We are determined that students who have trained under our leadership will first and foremost have servant hearts and kingdom values. Good theology is important,

careful and astute thinking is essential, but it is without value if
we do not live what we believe. In other words, the theory and
praxis we described in the introduction under the rubric of
practical theology are both important. Who we are and what
we do are both important.

We have also learnt that people are more important than
projects. Although we are still goal-oriented people and love to
achieve, we have determined that this will never be at the
expense of our relationship, our marriage, our children, grandchildren or our friendships. Some of those friendships were
forged in the heat of suffering and are too precious to fracture
now. Another lasting determination in our hearts is that faith
will always be more important than feelings. God gave us feelings
and we experienced a range of them beyond what we could
have imagined during the time of Jason's hospitalisation. However, we were equally as conscious during that time of something deep inside us that was more sustaining and more
meaningful than the rapidly changing feelings and emotions
that we were subject to. We learnt that this deep confidence in
a gracious God is real and it sustains.

And so we continue to live certain lives. We are secure in our
experience in time and certain that God will do all things well.
The end of the age is His business, but we live with eternity in
our hearts, sure, certain and blessed.

Endnotes

120. 1 Thessalonians 4:18
121. John 14:1-4
122. C. H. Dodd introduced the idea of a realised eschatology as a way of suggesting that Jesus was not overly concerned about the future.
123. Wright, *The Challenge of Jesus,* pp6-9; pp137-139. S. Hauerwas and W. H. Willimon, *Resident Aliens: A Provocative Christian Assessment of Culture and Ministry* (Nashville: TN: Abingdon Press, 1989), pp86-92.
124. Walsh and Keesmaat, *Colossians Remixed,* pp201-233. W. Brueggemann, *Deep Memory Exuberant Hope: Contested Truth in a Post-Christian World* (Minneapolis, MN: Fortress Press, 2000). W. Brueggeman, *The Prophetic Imagination* (Minneapolis, MN: Fortress Press, second edition, 2001).

Dying to Live

The paradox of Christian faith

"Courage is almost a contradiction of terms. It means a strong desire to live taking the form of readiness to die. The paradox of courage is that a man must be a little careless of his life even in order to keep it."
—G. K. Chesterton

"For to me, to live is Christ and to die is gain."
(Philippians 1:21)

Attempts have been made over the centuries to formulate Christian faith and doctrine. Most have been well intentioned with the goal of helping people understand how God works in human affairs. So we have created lengthy liturgies, developed a comprehensive church calendar and, more recently, described God's ways by means of spiritual laws or principles. Whole books have been written on the subject of five or even seven spiritual laws and the impression could be that by simply learning these few principles we can unravel the whole of God's plan for our lives.

If only it were that simple! It is wonderful to have a great array of good confessions and to declare a positive faith. Making known God's goodness and our expectations is a good thing to be celebrated. However, these confessions of faith only take on meaning when they are counterbalanced with deeply held convictions regarding our commitment to God no matter what. Somehow life does not always match the cliché the visiting preacher teaches or the catchy phrase of a new faith song. For each promise of God's blessing there must be a deep-seated attitude that faith will continue, even if there is no obvious outward sign of that blessing. Choices regarding constancy in faith and life are what really define our relationship with God – an unshakable courage that declares that God is amazing, even when life is not a marker of spiritual maturity.

This paradoxical element of faith is not something new.[125] In fact, at the very centre of the teaching of Jesus we discover these apparent conflicts. For example, Jesus teaches us that in order to live we must die.[126] In order to receive we must learn to give.[127] Faith actually operates best when it exists in a kind of creative tension. Imagine a bow and arrow. Neither the bow nor the arrow are of much use at all if there is no tension on the bowstring. As the archer pulls back on the bow and provides the string with tension, so an energy builds which, if the archer uses it creatively by pointing towards the target, enables the arrow to fly straight and true. So God allows creative tension to build in our lives. Sometimes it is by taking us through experiences that are challenging. At other times He may call on us to give sacrificially just when we are in need ourselves. Delayed gratification is a tool that God uses often in order to develop much greater character qualities such as patience, kindness and grace. Instant answers and quick solutions are not the currency of faith. Time and tension combine to allow God to produce something of lasting value.

We learnt elements of this paradoxical faith life quite literally some years ago. We have always been blessed with good health and fairly high energy levels. A lifetime of ministry cannot help but build resilience and strength. We have always enjoyed a rather simple faith by living with a daily gratitude for food, shelter and good health. Without any compromise to this faith we have also gladly engaged the medical profession when little things needed sorting out. Thus it was, when we first took up residence in the United States, that we took out appropriate health insurance. Completely trusting God and making provision for the help of the medical profession were safely bound up in the creative tension that we have described. There is no conflict for us – we are in the world even if we are not of the world.[128]

We have already described in chapter 14 how, after two years in the States, Paul became eligible for a "well man" health check – and the series of events that culminated in him undergoing very serious and major heart surgery. It was a painful journey of uncertainty mixed with faith. There was clearly a sense of peace that we knew came from our faith and our relationship with a caring and eternal God. But, there was also an uncertainty throughout this time, simply due to not knowing how things would turn out. Somehow the two coexisted in our hearts, both real and to some extent, both necessary. The one reminded us of the eternal promise of God the other of our humanity. The one sustained us through months of uncertainty whilst the medical specialists were trying to plan for major surgery. The other kept us dependent upon God and ensured that we lived every day to the full. The paradox of a complete blend of certainty and uncertainty, of peace and anxiety, and of an eternal perspective and time was before us on a daily basis and kept a creative tension that was ultimately producing something of great worth. That something was a greater love for life and for each other. It was an overwhelming sense of gratitude for each new day and a determination to live above pettiness.

When the day arrived for Paul's scheduled surgery in the UK, he worked his normal morning routine and returned home to be driven by Carol to the hospital. Our children, who both lived in the United States, had joined us by this time and so we prayed as a family and made our way the twenty or so miles to Sheffield. It was the first time that Paul had ever been admitted to hospital, but he settled in quickly and began talking to the others on the ward with him. He honestly thought that some of them would not make it through the night they looked so ill. After years of being a pastor the questions came easily and soon Paul was finding out what each of his friends in the ward were there for. It seemed as though most were about to have triple or quadruple bypasses. They had all been informed that their operations would last anything from two to four hours. This gave Paul great hope and he thought he would be in and out in a matter of an hour or two.

As previously recorded, later that day when the anaesthetist came to see Paul and ask some pre-operation questions, only then did it emerge that Paul was scheduled for fifteen hours of surgery. The procedure was so complex that, with his head packed in ice and careful monitoring the surgeons would be required to cut all life support – no respirator, no by-pass machine – and carry out the operation in a window of about twelve minutes, during which time Paul would be clinically dead. This should allow enough time to remove the faulty valve, replace it with a mechanical one and then insert a prosthetic aorta (a fancy name for a piece of plastic pipe!). The anaesthetist's closing, but obligatory, comments were about the risk of neurological damage that was particularly high with this procedure and the risk of death. It was not very comforting at all.

Paul was given some sleeping tablets and knew very little until about thirty-six hours later. Carol assures him that she came to him early the next morning and that he asked to pray for her and the family. Those long hours plunged Carol again into the tense world of faith blended with human emotions. The paradox of living with the deep inner assurance, knowing that God is in complete control of our lives, and the inevitable uncertainty of allowing time to run its course visited her again during this time. The hours went slowly by and eventually she was allowed into the intensive care unit to visit Paul. All the memories of Jason's time in hospital came flooding back and Carol was so grateful for the support of her brother Geoff and Anna and Jason. The operation was successful and Paul made a complete recovery. The outcome was excellent, the process agonising.

How typical this is of the faith-journey that Christ-followers take. The Bible reminds us that we do not carry on our struggles in the realm of humanity alone.[129] There is a greater world invisible to the human eye. It is a world that God rules over, but nevertheless has sinister forces at work within it. At times, these sinister forces can work directly or indirectly in our circumstances. However, the tapestry of New Testament teaching goes on to remind us that the power at work in us is greater than any sinister or evil power.[130] Nevertheless, it is the tension between these two that creates this paradoxical life that we live. We live in the *now* but the *not yet*. We live with deep and lasting certainty that God who starts a good work in us will see the work through to completion and yet the whole process can only be viewed as through a dark piece of glass.[131] The life of the committed Christ-follower is like watching a solar eclipse through very dark glasses. There is every evidence of the work of a gracious and loving God, but at times the borders of our vision become blurred and the image indistinct. We know, but will know more.[132]

After eight days Paul was allowed home. Nervously Carol drove the car as he clutched a little pillow to his chest. This was a new experience. Together we drove quietly out of the city and onto the country roads that lead to our home. At first Paul thought that he was suffering from some after effect of the drugs he had received. Emotion welled up as he saw the beautiful countryside. He bit his lower lip in an effort to contain the wave upon wave of feeling that began to flow over him. He saw beautiful hedgerows and striking, gnarled trees in the fields. Everything was more beautiful than he could ever remember seeing before. His eyes were hungry; it was as if he could not take enough in. Between quiet sobs and through freely flowing tears he understood again how good it was to be alive. For ten months the prospect of an early death had lingered just beneath the surface. Now there was the promise of life. The thought of returning home with the bride that he had married over thirty years before was beyond description. Life was rich, full and freely available. The prospect of hugging his children and then, in time, their children flooded Paul's heart and mind and produced deep gratitude. God was so kind, so good and so faithful. Those promptings that Carol had felt some years before were proven to be more than just the normal concern of a wife for her husband. The picture was now much more obvious. God had been at work, Carol had been sensitive to His leading and now we both knew why He had allowed this experience to take place.

For both of us, the experience was a graphic and powerful illustration of how God works. In order for the surgical procedure to be carried out Paul literally had to die. It was only when his heart was motionless that the surgery, which would give the prospect of a long and healthy life, could take place. Out of death, life sprang forth.

And so it is in all of our lives if we claim to be followers of Christ. The Apostle Paul had no doubt about living in this creative tension, this remarkable paradox. To live was Christ and to die was gain. This sets the Christ-follower apart. This amazing capacity to believe in miracles, but not to be discouraged if they do not happen is a mystery not worth trying to explain. In exactly the same way it allows us to experience miracles, but not lose our love for the routine. Paradoxical, creative tension – however we choose to explain it, this is the life of God in us. The capacity for mortals to be indwelt by the immortal God is a mystery and a wonder, but it is true nevertheless.[133] We find truth in the thought that we live, yet strangely, it is not we that live at all – it is Christ who is alive in us. The certain life is one that is found in dying to self in order that Christ might live in and through us, bringing hope to others, restoring what is broken and declaring life eternal.[134]

Endnotes

125. Hebrews 11:1: *"Now faith is being sure of what we hope for and certain of what we do not see."* Saint Augustine said, "Faith is to believe what you do not see; the reward for this faith is to see what you believe."

126. John 12:24-25. Gandhi said, "Live as if you were to die tomorrow. Learn as if you were to live forever."

127. Matthew 10:8; Luke 6:38; Acts 20:35

128. John 15:19

129. Ephesians 6:12

130. 1 John 4:4

131. Philippians 1:6; 1 Corinthians 13:12

132. 1 Corinthians 13: 12: *"Now I know in part; then I shall know fully, even as I am fully known."*

133. Colossians 1:27: *"To them God has chosen to make known among the Gentiles the glorious riches of this mystery, which is Christ in you, the hope of glory."*

134. Romans 6: 8: *"Now if we died with Christ, we believe that we will also live with Him."*

Can You Hear the Drums Beating?

A call to mission

"How, then, can they call on the one they have not believed in? And how can they hear without someone preaching to them?"
(Romans 10: 14)

"Then I heard the voice of the Lord saying, 'Whom shall I send and who will go for us?' And I said: ' Here am I, Send me!'"
(Isaiah 6:8)

Central to any discovery of the way and will of God for our lives is an understanding of the Bible. Christians believe fervently that the Bible paints a picture of the nature of God in such a way as to allow us to discover Him and His way for our lives. As mentioned time and again throughout these pages this means that we must approach the Bible in such a way as to prevent its misuse and abuse. We do not worship the Bible, but we do honour and respect its message. We do not use the Bible to substantiate our point of view, rather we adopt a point of view based upon a commitment to the whole Bible and its overarching stories. So, finding the will of God through quoting a single verse or reading some huge importance into one passage is a dangerous practice.

It is almost inevitable that we will gain a skewed theology if we do not take time to understand the central theme of the

Bible. In very simple terms it is this: God comes into relationship with human beings and then requires those same human beings to be His reflectors. This theme starts in the ancient history of the Bible where our first parents were to reflect God's order of things.[135] They were given the opportunity to enjoy creation, name animals and thus demonstrate the rule of heaven on earth.[136] The theme continues throughout the narrative. The loving nature of the eternal God reflects off the lives of faith-filled people such as Job, Noah, Abraham and other early patriarchs.

This "God-reflecting" concept is vitally important in understanding the relationship that God had with Israel as a whole.[137] His chosen people were not some form of exclusive community that had a monopoly on God. Quite the opposite, they were intended to be used by God to bring hope to nations and to demonstrate what life can really be like when you are part of a God-reflecting community. A careful reading of the prophetic books of the Bible show that God sends messengers with strong warnings when His people refuse to reflect Him and become selfish, nationalistic, uncaring or abusive of others.[138]

Put very simply, the whole of the Bible is a story of God's redemptive work in the earth and thus the only way to accurately interpret the Bible and live by its instruction is to understand this principle. Every distortion of biblical truth, every cultic or sect-like bit of behaviour inevitably develops when people use the Bible to support their own viewpoint, preach an exclusive kind of message, and believe that they are somehow superior to everyone else. We grew up in South Africa where we experienced daily the effects of an entire political system that was built on a distorted interpretation of the Bible, suggesting that it was God who ordained people to live separate from each other based on the colour of their skin.

This Bible theme of God-reflecting continues through the whole of the New Testament. When the angel announces to Mary that she will conceive and bear a son it was made clear that this child would be Emmanuel, God with us.[139] Jesus ministry is the most thrilling account of God-reflecting grace – blind people were healed, the deaf heard and the sick were made whole. A dramatic expression of justice was demonstrated, even to the point of the woman being caught in adultery having no accusers due to Christ's intervention.[140] Ultimately, Christ's life, death and resurrection demonstrated the massive commitment that God has to redeem human kind and reveal His love. In this sense, although He was God Himself, in His humanity Christ became the greatest of all God-reflectors. He is our great example.[141]

In the biblical record there are two more key principles to add to this brief summary of the greatest of all Bible themes. The first is the commission of Christ to go into all the world and make disciples.[142] This is a clarion call to reflect Him in all the nations – something that the early disciples clearly managed to do.[143] The second is the promise of one just like Jesus who would be sent to actually indwell us and empower us to be His witnesses or reflectors.[144] This is the Holy Spirit, who came powerfully on the day of Pentecost to indwell Christ-followers and continues to do exactly the same to the present day.[145] However we wish to expand on this theme or investigate specific portions of the Bible, the same message will condition our understanding of Scripture from beginning to end. It is the amazing message that God loves us, He has provided a way for us to know Him, and those who do know Him will reflect His character and nature wherever they are. Put another way, the Father sent the Son, the Father and Son sent the Spirit and now God the Father, Son and Holy Spirit send us to be bearers of good news wherever we are.[146]

This theme can be described in one word: *mission*. A certain life is lived with a commitment to the cause of Christ in the earth. Choices and values are impacted by the greater theme of

God's redemptive plan. Lifestyle is impacted more by our commitment to Him than our commitment to our own cultural perspective. Even reading our Bible is no longer a selfish devotion just to find out what God wants to do for me – it is now an exciting understanding of what He wants to do through me!

When our children were very young we began one of the most exciting adventures of our lives. As recorded earlier, we started a missionary training centre called Africa School of Missions. Soon after relocating to the new college campus, just outside of White River in South Africa, we had to contemplate our long term housing needs. Paul's father had died some months before and had left an inheritance to each of his children. We realised that there was enough money to either buy a comfortable home in White River or to invest in the vision that God had given us by providing the funds to build a home on campus. We acknowledged the fact that there would be no specific financial benefit to us in doing this, but we were also conscious that it would demonstrate the depth of our commitment to the vision God had given to us for training missionaries.

Thus, the choice was made and we gave the money to the college on the understanding that it would be used to build a house that we could use as our family home as long as we were based there. We had immense fun planning and supervising the building of that home and celebrated when the day came when we could move in to it with our young family.

After completing the building of the house and moving in, the father of one of our staff members visited the campus. He was not a Christ-follower and was clearly confused as he evaluated the sacrificial lifestyles of the faculty and staff of ASM. Late in the day of his visit he was introduced to Carol. Some how he had found out the story behind the financing of the home we were living in. He was not at all diplomatic in the way he spoke to Carol. He stated that, in his opinion, we had acted unwisely and even stated that the investing of our inheritance made us "idiots". He could not understand how we could make a decision that not only eroded our future potential wealth, but which would be disadvantageous to our children.

Feeling quite despondent after this unwelcome tirade Carol retreated to the relative sanctuary of our veranda. She went through some deep soul searching as she sat alone. Had we been irresponsible? What would we do when it came time to face the need to educate our children or face the prospect of retirement? As clearly as she could remember anything else that God had whispered to her through the years, she knew the voice of God in that moment. The deep reassurance in her heart was that if we were faithful in serving God and honouring His call upon our lives, He would always provide; we would lack nothing and all of our needs, both short and long term, would be met. We have not always had everything we wanted, but we have always had everything that we have needed. We still have some living to do, but if the faithfulness of God in our lives thus far is anything to go by, we are certain of a secure and sure future.

The college campus was situated in close proximity to a large and unplanned sprawl of rural housing that resulted from the horrible segregation policies of the government at the time. People were granted small parcels of land upon which they built meagre little homes. These homes were miles from any centre where work might be obtained and the land had little agricultural value, so thousands were condemned to poverty living in inadequate housing with no sanitation, running water or even basic services. We made contact with many church leaders in this area and the college did its best to provide meaningful employment to as many as possible. We began a number of community projects including sewing, car upholstery and very basic health care.

Although we became familiar with the area, there was one fairly disconcerting thing that resulted in living so close to it. Each night the local witch doctors would beat their drums for hours on end. In the quietness of the African countryside this sound could travel for miles and after an hour or so of consistent beating the sound would be almost hypnotic. We would plan for our children's bedtime, read a story or two and always tuck them in with a little time of prayer. One evening Anna asked us where the drumbeats came from and what they meant. We realised that we had never seriously thought about where they came from. The question troubled Carol for several days.

Several days later Carol felt a growing impulse to go and find just where the drumbeats were emanating from. She drove out of the college campus, down the main road and into one of the adjacent villages. There were a few women there and Carol tried to engage them in conversation. She later made contact with the pastor of a little church built into the hillside above the village. It was not long before she became overwhelmingly aware that there were not many adults around during the day. At the same time there were clearly many children. As her conversations continued she was shocked to discover that there were scores of little eight to ten year olds who could not attend school because they had to stay at home looking after much younger siblings. The story of her response to this desperately needy situation is recorded in chapter 10.

What this earlier chapter did not relate was just how costly this commitment to little boys and girls was going to be. The work was exhausting and then it became dangerous. At that time South Africa was facing a very challenging future politically. The Apartheid regime was desperately holding on to power and the grassroots revolution was becoming more militant. Communities such as the one in which Carol worked were ideal festering grounds for discontent. High unemployment, systemic poverty, dysfunctional families and society were all key ingredients in the growing anger against white rule. Young, discontented people, especially young men were encouraged to become "comrades" with the one stated goal of making the nation ungovernable. Unfortunately, all white people were viewed with suspicion and soon these young men turned their attention to Carol and the work she was doing in the village. Messages began to circulate that they were planning to burn the church with the "white woman" in it. On one occasion an angry group of young men surrounded Carol's vehicle as she was making her way home. She understood enough of the local dialect to know that they were shouting "kill the white woman!" Carol began to pray and ensured that she did not stop the engine. Inexplicably, they suddenly stood back making room for Carol to get through and drive home. She was understandably shaken, but felt undeterred. Before she could make her way back to the little corrugated church the next day the pastor walked across the hill and knocked on our front door. He pleaded with Carol not to return until the security situation improved. Broken-hearted, Carol respected his request and did not return that day.

We found out a few weeks later that the pastor had paid for this with his life. He had been poisoned and the church burnt down. There were probably other factors involved, but we mourned his death and felt a terrible sadness that the work could not continue. For months Carol advocated on behalf of the children and some larger agencies investigated what could be done. However, nothing was done and after several months it became obvious that the work simply could not continue. We continued to occupy ourselves with all the other open doors that God had given us and persisted in our call to train men and women in what was certainly one of the most isolated countries on earth at the time.

We remember well the lunchtime news report that Nelson Mandela was to be set free from prison and the African National Congress un-banned. There followed several years of negotiations and eventually, in almost a miraculous way, South Africa transitioned to a fully-fledged democracy in 1994. Within weeks the political climate changed and opportunities in the locality where Carol had previously worked were presented once again.

South African missionaries could travel more freely and we were amazed to see students from Africa School of Missions serving in well over fifty different nations. Primary health care projects were continued and eventually home-based care for those suffering from HIV/AIDS were initiated. The seeds that had been faithfully planted over a ten year period were now starting to bear much fruit. There is still a great amount of need. A new government has helped much in the provision of clean water and electricity and the area where Carol began her work is now better serviced, relatively speaking. However, the HIV/AIDS pandemic soon hit that area and today thousands are suffering as a result. Now, many of the children are not looking after their younger siblings because their parents are at work, but because their patents are dead. We still return to that area. Now we take teams of our students from the UK and paint orphan's bedrooms, dig foundations for centres that feed them and join with dedicated health workers as they visit homes ravaged by a cruel disease. We still advocate, we still ache, but a commitment to the poorest and the most needy is actually what gives us such certain lives.

As simply as we know how the message of our lives is this: they are certain! Certain in that we desire to live with a sense of purpose, knowing that we have a unique and special reason for living, even when times are uncertain. But certain also in the sense of living with an internal security and a spiritual joy that springs from knowing God and making Him known. We recommend this certain life. We look back at this journey that we have taken with deep gratitude whilst looking forward with immense anticipation.

It is unavoidable that a call to mission will always involve two dimensions, much like the rails of a railway track. On the one hand there is the exhilaration of God-encounters. These are the indescribable moments when you become aware that God is going to use you. It is in these moments that the human heart experiences the thrill of discovering a sense of destiny and purpose. Along with this is the deep reassurance of God's faithfulness and the promise of His provision. However, running parallel to this amazing involvement of God in our lives is the reality of living in a dark and sometimes dangerous world. Sacrifice, commitment and cost are all part of the journey. Spanning these two dimensions can be difficult and, at times, painful, but the end result is always amazing.

We never stop listening for the drum beat. We do not want to miss any opportunity that comes our way. Our ears are constantly open to hear where the next drum beat is coming from and how we can partner with God in bringing transformation to some other part of the world, some other community. This is the calling of every Christian person. We are called to live as pilgrims because ultimately this earth is not our home. For us that has sometimes meant the heartache of leaving mother, father, siblings, our children and our grandchildren. We cannot say that this has always been easy. What we can say is that through every stage of our journey our loving Father has walked with us and given us grace for every situation. He has also made it possible for us to see our children and our beautiful little granddaughter, Ava, regularly. He has blessed us with two amazing children who have always been incredibly unselfish. They have always willingly, from the time they were young, released us to ministry. We enjoy a wonderful relationship with both of them as well as our son-in-law, Rich. Ava (Anna and Rich's daughter) is only 16 months old at the time of writing and she has given us untold joy. Now her little brother, Tylan, is on his way and if everything goes to plan he will arrive at the end of January 2011. What blessed and certain lives we have lived.

We trust that you too will take meaningful decisions, evaluate choices carefully and live in such a way as to demonstrate a certain life. In so doing, the Bible will come alive with meaning, the will and way of God will be easier to discern, relationships will be more functional and the good news of God's love will impact needy people everywhere. This is the fruit of a certain life!

Endnotes

135. Genesis 1:27
136. Genesis 2
137. Exodus 8:22, 9:16; Leviticus 20:22-24, 22:31, 26:3-13
138. Isaiah 1:16-18, 10:1-3, 32:7-8; Ezekiel 22:29-30; Hosea 12:7-14; Amos 2:6-7, 5:7, 6:12; Micah 6:1-12.
139. Matthew 1:20-23; Luke 1:26-38
140. John 8:1-11. See also John 4.
141. John 13:15.
142. Matthew 28:18-20
143. The book of Acts is a wonderful account of the works of Jesus' followers.
144. John 14:15-21
145. Acts 2:1-13
146. Two authors that expounded the doctrine of the *missio Dei* are the late South African Missiologist David Bosch and the late missionary Lesslie Newbigin. Their books are worth a read. D. J. Bosch, *Transforming Mission* and D. J. Bosch, *Believing in the Future: Toward a Missiology of Western Culture* (Harrisburg, PA: Trinity Press International, 1995). L. Newbigin, *Foolishness to the Greeks: The Gospel and Western Culture* (Grand Rapids, MI: Eerdmans, 1986.) L. Newbigin, *The Open Secret: An Introduction to the Theology of Mission* (Grand Rapids: MI: Eerdmans, revised edition, 1995). L. Newbigin, *A Word in Season: Perspectives on Christian World Missions* (Grand Rapids, MI: Eerdmans, 1995).

Bibliography

R. S. Anderson, *The Shape of Practical Theology: Empowering Ministry with Theological Praxis* (Downers Grove: Intervarsity Press, 2001).

D. S. Browning, *A Fundamental Practical Theology: Descriptive and Strategic Proposals* (Minneapolis, MN: Fortress Press, 1996).

D. J. Bosch, *Believing in the Future: Toward a Missiology of Western Culture* (Harrisburg, PA: Trinity Press International, 1995).

D. J. Bosch, *Transforming Mission: Paradigm Shifts in Theology of Mission* (Maryknoll, NY: Orbis, 1991).

G. Boyd, *The Myth of a Christian Nation: How the Quest for Political Power is Destroying the Church* (Grand Rapids: Zondervan, 2005).

W. Brueggemann, *Deep Memory Exuberant Hope: Contested Truth in a Post-~Christian World* (Minneapolis, MN: Fortress Press, 2000).

W. Brueggemann, *The Prophetic Imagination* (Minneapolis: Fortress Press, second edition, 2002).

N. Cole, *The Organic Church: Growing Faith Where Life Happens* (San Francisco, CA: Jossey-Bass, 2005).

E. Dyck (Ed.) *The Act of Reading the Bible: A Multi-Disciplinary Approach to Biblical Interpretation* (Downers Grove: InterVarsity Press, 1996).

D. G. Fee and D. Stuart, *How to Read the Bible For all its Worth: A Guide to Understanding the Bible* (Grand Rapids: Zondervan, 1993).

D. G. Fee and D. Stuart, *How to Read the Bible Book by Book: A Guided Tour* (Grand Rapids: Zondervan, 2002).

M. Frost, *Exiles: Living Missionally in a Post Christian Culture* (Peabody, Massachusetts: Hendrickson Publishers, 2006).

M. Frost and A. Hirsch, *ReJesus: A Wild Messiah for a Missional Church* (Peabody, Massachusetts: Hendrickson Publishers, 2009).

S. Grenz, *Theology for the Community of God* (Grand Rapids, MI: Eerdmans, 1994).

O. Guinness, *The Call: Finding and Fulfilling the Central Purpose of your Life* (Nashville, Tennessee: Word Publishing, 1998).

A. Hirsch, *The Forgotten Ways* (Grand Rapids: Brazos Press, 2006).

R. Hattersley, *John Wesley: A Brand from the Burning* (London: Little Brown, reprinted 2003).

S. Hauerwas, *A Community of Character: Toward a Constructive Social Ethic* (Notre Dame, IN: University of Notre Dame Press, 1981).

P. Jenkins, *The Next Christendom: the Coming of Global Christianity* (Oxford: Oxford University press, 2002).

J. H. Kane, *A Concise History of the Christian World Mission: A Panoramic View of Missions from Pentecost to the Present* (Grand Rapids: Baker Academic, 1978).

D. MacCulloch, *The Reformation: A History* (New York: Penguin Group, 2003).

A. Macintyre, *After Virtue: A Study in Moral Theory* (Notre Dame, IN: University of Notre Dame Press, second edition, 1984).

L. Newbigin, *Foolishness to the Greeks: The Gospel and Western Culture* (Grand Rapids: Eerdmans, 1986).

L. Newbigin, *A Word in Season: Perspectives on Christian World Missions* (Grand Rapids, MI: Eerdmans, 1995.)

L. Newbigin, *The Open Secret: An Introduction to the Theology of Mission* (Grand Rapids: MI: Eerdmans, revised edition, 1995).

R. R. Osmer, *Practical Theology: An Introduction* (Grand Rapids, MI: Eerdmans, 2008).

H. Peskett and V. Ramachandra, *the Message of Mission: The Glory of Christ in all Time and Space* (Leicester: InterVarsity Press, 2003).

A. M. Renwick and A.M Harman, *The Story of the Church* (Downers Grove: InterVarsity Press, third edition, 2004).

L. Sanneh, *Whose Religion is Christianity? The Gospel Beyond the West* (Grand Rapids: Eerdmans, 2003).

M. Scott Peck, *The Road Less Travelled: A New Psychology of Love, Traditional Values and Spiritual Growth* ((New York: Simon and Schuster, 1978).

J. K. Smith, *A Radical Orthodoxy: Mapping a Post-secular Theology* (Grand Rapids, MI: Baker Academic, 2004).

P. Tickle, *The Great Emergence: How Christianity is Changing and Why* (Grand Rapids, MI: Baker Books, 2009).

M. Volf, *Exclusion & Embrace: A Theological Exploration of Identity, Otherness and Reconciliation* (Nashville, TN: Abingdon Pres, 1996).

M. Volf, *Free of Charge: Giving and Forgiving in a Culture Stripped of Grace* (Grand Rapids: Zondervan, 2005).

M. Volf, *The End of Memory: Remembering Rightly in a Violent World* (Grand Rapids: Eerdmans, 2006).

P. Ward, *Selling Worship: How What We Sing Has Changed the Church* (London: SCM Press, 2005).

P. Ward, *Participation and Mediation: A Practical Theology for the Liquid Church* (London: SCM Press, 2008).

A. F. Walls, *the Missionary Movement in Christian History: Studies in the Transmission of Faith* (Maryknoll: Orbis Books, 2005).

B. J. Walsh and S.C. Keesmaat, *Colossians Remixed: Subverting the Empire* (Downers Grove: IL: InterVarsity Press, 2004).

R. E. Webber, *Ancient Future Faith: Rethinking Evangelicalism for a Postmodern World* (Grand Rapids: Baker Books, 1999).

R. E. Webber, *The Younger Evangelicals: Facing the Challenges of the New World* (Grand Rapids: Baker Books, 2002).

D. Willard, *Knowing Christ Today: Why We Can Trust Spiritual Knowledge* (New York, NY: HarperCollins Publishers, 2009).

W. H. Willimon, *Resident Aliens: A Provocative Christian Assessment of Culture and Ministry* (Nashville: TN: Abingdon Press, 1989).

N. T. Wright, *The Challenge of Jesus* (London: SPCK, 2000).

T. Wright, *Simply Christian* (London: SPCK, 2006).

T. Wright, *Surprised by Hope* (London: SPCK, 2007).